The Truman Years

1 9 4 5 - 1 9 5 3

Teachers Guide

*A Supplemental Teaching Unit
from the Records of the National Archives*

NATIONAL
ARCHIVES

National Archives Trust Fund Board
National Archives and Records Administration

A B C ⬥ C L I O

ABC – CLIO, Inc
130 Cremona Drive, P.O. Box 1911
Santa Barbara, CA 93116-1911
ISBN 1-57607-789-6

WAR DEPARTMENT
PUBLIC RELATIONS DIVISION
PRESS SECTION
Tel. RE 6700

Other Units in this Series:

December 31, 1946

STATEMENT OF SECRETARY OF WAR PATTERSON
ON TRANSFER OF MANHATTAN DISTRICT

With the transfer of responsibility for the Nation's atomic energy program from the War Department to the U. S. Atomic Energy Commission, we will have carried out the long range plans of President Roosevelt, President Truman, Secretary Stimson, and General Marshall, who months before Hiroshima clearly recognized that Congress should create an independent agency of the government to carry on this vital work.

The War Department has consistently supported the principle of civilian control of atomic energy in its broad aspects, and we look forward to a relationship with the Atomic Energy Commission that will be of mutual advantage. I want to pledge to Chairman Lilienthal, Doctor Bacher, Mr. Pike, Mr. Strauss, and Mr. Waymack the continuing wholehearted cooperation and support of the War Department.

The Commission is taking over a well organized and efficient activity. General Groves has maintained the Manhattan District in a state of readiness for transfer to the Commission, and he has directed its operations with an efficiency and effectiveness consistent with the highest ideals of the Service. I want to take this opportunity to pay tribute to him once more for his outstanding contribution to the security and welfare of the nation, and to commend him for his continuing devotion to duty in a position for which he has already been awarded the Army's highest award for this type of service, the Distinguished Service Medal.

END

DISTRIBUTION: Aa, Af, B, D (except Do), E, Ea, Ma, N, Sc, T.
10:00 A.M.

Table of Contents

Foreword

In its efforts to make the historical records of the federal government available nationally, the National Archives began a program in 1970 to introduce these vast resources to secondary school students. School classes visiting the National Archives in Washington were given the opportunity to examine and interpret original sources as historians use them. Teachers and students responded enthusiastically and encouraged the development of a series of supplemental teaching units.

The Truman Years: 1945-1953 is the eighth unit in the series. It, like those that have preceded and will follow, is intended to bring you and your students the excitement and satisfaction of working with primary sources and to enhance your instructional program.

FRANK G. BURKE
Acting Archivist of the United States
1986

...to bring you and your students the excitement and satisfaction of working with primary sources and to enhance your instructional program.

Preface

◆ This unit is made up of 11 exercises.

◆ Each exercise includes reproductions of documents from the National Archives and suggests classroom activities based on these documents.

The Truman Years: 1945-1953 is a teaching unit designed to supplement your students' study of the post-World War II period. The unit is made up of 11 exercises. Each exercise includes reproductions of documents from the National Archives and suggests classroom activities based on these documents. The documents include official correspondence, telegrams, photographs, political cartoons, pamphlets, maps, and court decisions. Students practice the historian's skills as they complete exercises, using these documents to gather information, identify points of view, evaluate evidence, form hypotheses, and draw conclusions.

The documents in this unit do not reflect every topic usually included in a history textbook. We consciously decided to omit documents pertaining to the conduct and conclusion of World War II. We made this decision because educators have requested that we focus on issues of the postwar era where there is a scarcity of primary sources. In some instances the federal government had no interest or authority over a given event and therefore compiled no records on it. In other cases documents in the National Archives on several historic topics proved to be difficult to use in the classroom due to the recent nature of the documents.

The Truman Years: 1945-1953 is useful in the government classroom as well as the history classroom. Activities included in exercises 1, 4, 6, 7, and 8 are designed specifically for use by government and civics teachers.

National Archives education specialists Wynell Burroughs Schamel and Jean M. West and education branch chief Elsie Freeman Finch developed this publication. We are pleased to issue a revised and updated set of these documentary teaching materials.

WYNELL B. SCHAMEL
LEE ANN POTTER
Education Specialists
2001

The Truman Years: 1945-1953 is a teaching unit designed to supplement your students' study of the post-World War II period.

$\mathcal{A}$cknowledgments

Many people helped in the original production of this unit. They include National Archives staff members Bonnie Baldwin, Dennis Bilger, Mark Corristan, Joseph Fernandez, Cindy Fox, Leslie Gray, Janet Hargett, Chauncey Jessup, Warren Ohrvall, Diane Palmer, Jimmy Rush, Amy Schmidt, Pauline Testerman, Les Waffen, Theresa Wertan, and Dale Whittaker.

Jack Holliday, a classroom teacher in Kettering, OH, and other social studies teachers reviewed elements of this unit. Their reactions and comments shaped and improved the document selection and the teaching exercises.

Edith James, Director of the Exhibits and Educational Programs Division; David Kepley, archivist in the Legislative Records Division; Pauline Testerman, audiovisual archives technician, Harry S. Truman Presidential Library; and Benedict Zobrist, Director of the Harry S. Truman Presidential Library, reviewed the unit for historical content.

During the republication process, we were ably assisted by George Mason University intern Adam Jevec; volunteers Elizabeth S. Lourie, Jane Douma Pearson, and Donald Alderson; and National Archives staff members Michael Hussey, A.J. Daverede, Patrick Osborn, Amy Patterson, Kate Flaherty, Donald Roe, and Charles Mayn.

𝒫ublisher's Note

Primary source documents have long been a cornerstone of ABC-CLIO's commitment to producing high-quality, learner-centered history and social studies resources. When our nation's students have the opportunity to interact with the undiluted artifacts of the past, they can better understand the breadth of the human experience and the present state of affairs.

It is with great enthusiasm that we celebrate the release of this series of teaching units designed in partnership with the National Archives—materials that we hope will bring historical context and deeper knowledge to U.S. middle and high school students. Each unit has been revised and updated, including new bibliographic references. Each teaching unit has been correlated to the curriculum standards for the teaching of social studies and history developed by the National Council for the Social Studies and the National Center for History in the Schools.

For more effective use of these teaching units in the classroom, each booklet is accompanied by an interactive CD-ROM which includes exercise worksheets, digital images of original documents, and, for four titles, sound recordings. A videocassette of motion pictures accompanies the teaching unit *The United States At War: 1944*. For those who would like to order facsimiles of primary source documents in their original sizes, or additional titles in this series, we have included an order form to make it easy for you to do so.

The mission of the National Archives is "to ensure ready access to the essential evidence that documents the rights of American citizens, the actions of Federal officials, and the national experience."

These units go a long way toward fulfilling that mission, helping the next generation of American citizens develop a clear understanding of the nation's past and a firm grasp of the role of the individual in guiding the nation's future. ABC-CLIO is honored to be part of this process.

BECKY SNYDER
Publisher & Vice President
ABC-CLIO Schools

The mission of the National Archives is "to ensure ready access to the essential evidence that documents the rights of American citizens, the actions of Federal officials, and the national experience."

Teaching With Documents Curriculum Standards Correlations

The National Council for the Social Studies and the National Center for History in the Schools have developed a set of comprehensive curriculum standards for the teaching of social studies and history. Take a look at how thoroughly the Teaching With Documents series supports the curriculum.

National Council for the Social Studies

	The Constitution: Evolution of a Government	The Bill of Rights: Evolution of Personal Liberties	The United States Expands West: 1785–1842	Westward Expansion: 1842–1912	The Civil War: Soldiers and Civilians	The Progressive Years: 1898–1917	World War I: The Home Front	The 1920's	The Great Depression and The New Deal World	War II: The Home Front	The United States At War: 1944	The Truman Years: 1945–1953	Peace and Prosperity: 1953–1961
CULTURE—should provide for the study of culture and cultural diversity	●	●	●	●	●			●		●			●
TIME, CONTINUITY & CHANGE—should provide for the study of the ways people view themselves in and over time	●	●	●	●	●	●	●	●	●	●	●		
PEOPLE, PLACES & ENVIRONMENT—should provide for the study of people, places, and environments	●	●	●	●	●			●	●				
INDIVIDUAL DEVELOPMENT & IDENTITY—should provide for the study of individual development and identity	●	●	●	●	●	●	●	●	●				●
INDIVIDUALS, GROUPS & INSTITUTIONS—should provide for the study of interactions among individuals, groups, and institutions	●	●	●	●	●	●		●	●		●	●	●
POWER, AUTHORITY & GOVERNANCE—should provide for the study of how structures of power are created and changed	●	●	●	●	●	●		●	●			●	●
PRODUCTION, DISTRIBUTION & CONSUMPTION—should provide for the study of the usage of goods and services	●		●	●	●	●		●	●			●	
SCIENCE, TECHNOLOGY & SOCIETY—should provide for the study of relationships among science, technology, and society	●	●	●	●	●			●			●	●	●
GLOBAL CONNECTIONS—should provide for the study of global connections and interdependence	●		●	●		●					●	●	●
CIVIC IDEALS & PRACTICES—should provide for the study of the ideals, principles, and practices of citizenship	●	●						●			●		

National Center for History in the Schools

	The Constitution: Evolution of a Government	The Bill of Rights: Evolution of Personal Liberties	The United States Expands West: 1785–1842	Westward Expansion: 1842–1912	The Civil War: Soldiers and Civilians	The Progressive Years: 1898–1917	World War I: The Home Front	The 1920's	The Great Depression and The New Deal World	War II: The Home Front	The United States At War: 1944	The Truman Years: 1945–1953	Peace and Prosperity: 1953–1961
CHRONOLOGICAL THINKING	●	●	●	●	●	●	●	●	●	●	●	●	●
HISTORICAL COMPREHENSION	●	●	●	●	●	●	●	●	●	●	●	●	●
HISTORICAL ANALYSIS & INTERPRETATION	●	●	●	●	●	●	●	●	●	●	●	●	●
HISTORICAL RESEARCH CAPABILITIES	●	●	●	●	●	●	●	●	●	●	●	●	●
HISTORICAL ISSUES-ANALYSIS & DECISION-MAKING	●	●	●	●	●	●	●	●	●	●	●	●	●

Introduction

This unit contains three elements: 1) a book, which contains a teachers guide and a set of reproductions of print documents, and 2) a CD-ROM, which contains the exercise worksheets from the teachers guide, a set of reproductions of print documents, and sound recordings in electronic format. In selecting the documents, we applied three standards. First, the documents must be entirely from the holdings of the National Archives and must reflect the actions of the federal government or citizens' responses to those actions. Second, each document must be typical of the hundreds of records of its kind relating to its particular topic. Third, the documents must be legible or audible and potentially useful for vocabulary development. In selecting documents we attempted to choose those having appeal to young people.

Objectives

We have provided an outline of the general objectives for the unit. You will be able to achieve these objectives by completing several, if not all, of the exercises in the unit. Because each exercise aims to develop skills defined in the general objectives, you may be selective and still develop those skills. In addition, each exercise has its own specific objectives.

UNIT CONTAINS:

- ◆ **1)** a book, which contains a teachers guide and a set of reproductions of print documents, and

- ◆ **2)** a CD-ROM, which contains the exercise worksheets from the teachers guide, a set of reproductions of print documents, and sound recordings in electronic format.

Outline

This unit on the Truman years includes 11 exercises, 9 of which relate to issues and trouble spots of the postwar period. Exercise 9 focuses on the personal and political life of President Truman, and exercise 11 is a photographic study of life in postwar America.

List of Documents

The list of documents gives specific information (e.g. date and name of author) and record group number for each document. Records in the National Archives are arranged in record groups. A typical record group (RG) consists of the records created or accumulated by a department, agency, bureau, or other administrative unit of the federal government. Each record group is identified for retrieval purposes by a record group number; for example, RG 218 (U.S. Joint Chiefs of Staff) or RG 227 (Office of Scientific Research and Development). Complete archival citations of all documents are listed in the appendix, p. 63.

Exercise Summary Chart

The chart shows the organization of the 11 exercises. For each exercise the chart outlines the materials needed, the document content, the student activities that are emphasized, the number of class periods needed, and the student ability levels for which the exercise has been designed. Review the chart carefully and decide which exercises to use based on your objectives for the students, their ability levels, and the content you wish to teach. The exercises may be adapted to fit your objectives and teaching style.

Introductory Exercises

Before starting exercises 1-11, it is important to familiarize students with documents and their importance to the historian who interprets them and writes history from them. We suggest that you direct students to do one or all of the introductory exercises. The Historian's Tools, p. 11, is designed to increase students' awareness of the process of analyzing historical information and is most appropriate for students working at or above ninth grade reading level. The Written Document Analysis, p. 13, is designed to help students analyze systematically any written document in this unit. The Photograph Analysis, p. 14, can be used for the same purpose with any of the photographs in the unit. The Cartoon Analysis, p. 17, can be used to analyze systematically political cartoons. The Sound Recording Analysis, p. 15, can be used to help students listen to sound recordings to retrieve historical information.

Classroom Exercises

This unit contains 11 suggested exercises. Within the explanatory material for each of the exercises, you will find the following information:

- ➤ Note to the teacher
- ➤ Classroom time required
- ➤ Objectives (specific)
- ➤ Materials needed
- ➤ Procedures
- ➤ Student worksheets

You may choose to combine several exercises on a topic within the unit. In some instances a document is used in more than one exercise when appropriate to the skill or content objectives. We encourage you to select and adapt the exercises and documents that best suit your own teaching style.

Ability Levels

As in our other units, we have developed exercises for students of different abilities. For some topics, we have designed two or more procedures, tailored to different student needs. Throughout the unit we have made an effort to provide exercises in which students utilize a variety of skills, including reading for understanding, interpreting maps and cartoons, and analyzing legislation and court cases. All lessons have procedures for ability levels one, two, and three. Procedures begin with strategies designed for level three students, continue with level two strategies, and conclude with level one strategies. Our definition of each ability level is as follows:

Level One: Good reading skills, ability to organize and interpret information from several sources with minimal direction from teacher, and ability to complete assignments independently.

Level Two: Average reading skills, ability to organize and interpret information from several sources with general direction from teacher, and ability to complete assignments with some assistance from teacher.

Level Three: Limited reading skills, and ability to organize and interpret information from several sources with step-by-step direction from teacher, and ability to complete assignments with close supervision from teacher.

These ability levels are merely guides. We recognize that you will adapt the exercises to suit your students' needs and your own teaching style.

Time Line

A time line is included for use by your students. You may want to reproduce it for each student or display it.

Bibliography

As students work with the documents, they should be assigned appropriate readings from their text and other secondary sources. They should also be encouraged to use the resources of school and public libraries. To guide them, an annotated bibliography appears at the end of the Teachers Guide.

General Objectives

Upon successfully completing the exercises in this unit, students should be able to demonstrate the following skills using a single document:

➤ Identify factual evidence

➤ Identify points of view (bias and/or prejudice)

➤ Collect, reorder, and weigh the significance of evidence

➤ Develop defensible inferences, conclusions, and generalizations from factual information

Using several documents from this unit, students should be able to:

➤ Analyze the documents to compare and contrast evidence

➤ Evaluate and interpret evidence drawn from the documents

Everything Unified, Everybody Happy

Outline of Classroom Exercises

The Truman Years: 1945-1953

Exercise 1
The Beginning of the Atomic Age

Exercise 2
The Conversion from War to Peace

Exercise 3
Cold War and Containment

Exercise 4
Civilian Control of the Military

Exercise 5
The Marshall Plan

Exercise 6
Israel and the Middle East

Exercise 7
Soviet Espionage and an Atmosphere of Distrust

Exercise 8
The Korean War

Exercise 9
Harry S. Truman

Exercise 10
Civil Rights

Exercise 11
Life in Postwar America: A Photographic Study

List of Documents

Following the identifying information for each document reproduced in the unit, we have given the record group (RG) number in which the original can be found. Should you want copies of these documents or, for other reasons, wish to refer to them in correspondence with us, give the complete archival citation, which is found in the appendix on page 63. **You may duplicate any documents in this unit for use with your students.**

Documents in *The Truman Years: 1945-1953* are taken from the following record groups: General Records of the U.S. Government (RG 11), District Courts of the United States (RG 21), United States Senate (RG 46), General Records of the Department of State (RG 59), Office of the Chief of Engineers (RG 77), War Department General and Special Staffs (RG 165), Office of Price Administration (RG 188), National Archives Collection of Donated Materials, Office of War Information (RG 208), U.S. Joint Chiefs of Staff (RG 218), Office of Scientific Research and Development (RG 227), Committee on Fair Employment Practice (RG 228), Supreme Court of the United States (RG 267), United States Information Agency (RG 306), Atomic Energy Commission (RG 326), and Office of the Secretary of Defense (RG 330). Additional documents are taken from the holdings of the Harry S. Truman Presidential Library.

1. Alvarez's notes and drawings of the first atomic explosion, July 16, 1945 (RG 227).

2. Groves' memo to Chief of Staff regarding third atomic bomb, August 10, 1945 (RG 77).

3. Photograph of a civil defense drill, n.d. (Harry S. Truman Presidential Library).

4. Commander in Chief Far East memo to War Department regarding interrogation of Japanese generals, February 10, 1947 (RG 165).

5. Green's letter to Truman about the Taft-Hartley Act, June 7, 1947 (Harry S. Truman Presidential Library).

6. Pamphlet about the cost of living of student veterans, December 1947 (Harry S. Truman Presidential Library).

7. Telegram about the Berlin blockade and airlift, June 27, 1948 (RG 218).

8. News column about Taft's opposition to NATO, July 11, 1949 (Harry S. Truman Presidential Library).

9. Senator Johnson's letter to Dean Acheson supporting recognition of the People's Republic of China, October 26, 1949 (RG 59).

10. Senator Smith's letter to Dean Acheson opposing recognition of the People's Republic of China, November 5, 1949 (RG 59).

11. Pamphlet about the Point Four program, 1950 (Harry S. Truman Presidential Library).

12. Senate Resolution 243, March 22, 1950 (Harry S. Truman Presidential Library).

13. War Department press release about transfer of the atomic energy program to the Atomic Energy Commission, December 31, 1946 (RG 326).

14. Cartoon, "Everything Unified, Everybody Happy," January 18, 1947 (Harry S. Truman Presidential Library). © Washington *Evening Star*. Used with permission.

15. Bradley's memo to MacArthur relieving him of command, April 11, 1951 (RG 218).

16. Cartoon, "Who does Truman think he is — the PRESIDENT?", by Jacob Burck; 1951 (Harry S. Truman Presidential Library). Reprinted with special permission from the Chicago *Sun-Times, Inc.* © 2001.

17. European Recovery Act of 1948 (Marshall Plan), January 6, 1948 (RG 11).

18. Cartoon, "Making Progress," April 10, 1949 (RG 218). © *Tampa Tribune*. Used with permission.

19. Annotated statement by Truman recognizing Israel, May 14, 1948 (Harry S. Truman Presidential Library).

20. Map of Israel's military situation, June 11, 1948 (RG 218).

21. Photograph, "Dr. Ralph Bunche at Arab-Israeli armistice talks," 1949 (RG 306). © by Bettmann Newsphotos. Used with permission.

22. Senator McCarthy's letter to Senator Tydings about loyalty investigations, June 3, 1950 (RG 46).

23. Cartoon, "Are You a Communist?", n.d. (Harry S. Truman Presidential Library). © Providence, RI, *Bulletin*. Used with permission.

24. Court order denying the Rosenbergs' application for a stay of execution, December 10, 1952 (RG 267).

25. Chart of quantitative reportage on the Rosenberg trial and related espionage topics, 1952 (RG 267).

26. Teletype of Truman's authorization of military intervention in Korea, June 27, 1950 (RG 218).

27. Proclamation by Truman of a national emergency, December 16, 1950 (RG 11).

28. Joint Chiefs of Staff memo to Secretary of Defense regarding Korean armistice proposals, March 27, 1951 (RG 330).

29. Photograph of President Truman campaigning in California, September 24, 1948 (Harry S. Truman Presidential Library).

30. Cartoon, "— and on Two Legs," November 3, 1948 (Harry S. Truman Presidential Library). © *Evansville Courier*. Used with permission.

31. Suarez's letter to Truman about the attempted assassination, November 8, 1950 (Harry S. Truman Presidential Library).

32. Booth's letter to Hewes regarding minority employment conditions in Los Angeles, March 15, 1946 (RG 228).

33. Executive Order No. 9981, July 26, 1948 (RG 11).

34. Photograph of Jackie Robinson, 1950 (RG 306). © Bettmann Newsphotos. Used with permission.

35. "Rests With Other Heroes; Indian Sergeant Is Buried in Dignity, With All Honor," *The Cincinnati Enquirer*, September 5, 1951 (Harry S. Truman Presidential Library).

36. Photograph of a housing project, 1946 (Harry S. Truman Presidential Library).

37. Photograph of the interior of prefabricated government housing, May 3, 1949 (Harry S. Truman Presidential Library). Reprinted by permission of the William H. Harmon Corporation of Wilmington, DE.

38. Advertisement for television, February 13, 1950 (Harry S. Truman Presidential Library). © Motorola Inc. Used with permission. [Note: Motorola sold its television business in the 1970s and now concentrates on high-technology industrial electronics.]

39. Advertisement for Lustron home, 1950 (Harry S. Truman Presidential Library).

40. Photograph of Erikson Oil Products station, North Lyndale, Minneapolis, December 29, 1954 (RG 21, Branch Archives, Kansas City, MO).

Sound Recordings on CD-ROM

Sound recording A. Musical program in support of continuation of the Office of Price Administration, 1946 (RG 188).

Sound recording B. "Iron Curtain" speech by Winston Churchill, March 6, 1946 (RG 208).

Sound recording C. "Truman Doctrine" speech by Harry S. Truman, March 12, 1947 (National Archives Collection of Donated Materials).

Sound recording D. Broadcast summary of Ronald Reagan testimony before the House Un-American Activities Committee, October 23, 1947 (National Archives Collection of Donated Materials).

Sound recording E. "Marshall Plan" speech by George C. Marshall, June 5, 1947 (National Archives Collection of Donated Materials).

Sound recording F. Broadcast summary of Alger Hiss testimony before the House Un-American Activities Committee, August 5, 1948 (National Archives Collection of Donated Materials).

Sound recording G. Combat actuality recording by Wes MacPheron in Korea, October 20, 1950 (RG 330).

Exercise Summary Chart

	EXERCISE	NUMBER OF DOCUMENTS	CONTENT	STUDENT ACTIVITIES	NUMBER OF CLASS PERIODS
1.	The Beginning of the Atomic Age Documents 1-3 and 13 Photograph Analysis worksheet	4	Military and civil impact of atomic technology	Analyzing photographs Using creative writing skills Researching from community sources	2-3
2.	The Conversion from War to Peace Documents 4-6 Sound recording A Worksheet 1	3	Postwar domestic legislation War crimes trials	Interpreting graphs Interpreting a sound recording Working in groups Comparing and contrasting domestic legislation between two eras	1-2
3.	Cold War and Containment Documents 7-12 Sound recordings B and C Worksheet 2	6	Postwar foreign policies and programs	Brainstorming Role-playing Analyzing documents and coming to conclusions Identifying point of view Interpreting a sound recording	2-4
4.	Civilian Control of the Military Documents 13-16 Worksheet 3	4	Postwar relations between civilian and military authorities	Interpreting cartoons Writing a position paper Reading for main ideas	2-3
5.	The Marshall Plan Documents 17 and 18 Sound recording E Sound Recording Analysis worksheet Worksheet 4	2	The Marshall Plan and the foreign policy of containment	Interpreting a cartoon Interpreting a sound recording Identifying cause and effect	1
6.	Israel and the Middle East Documents 19-21 Worksheet 5	3	U.S. policy in the Middle East	Interpreting a map Establishing a chronology Researching related topics	1-2

EXERCISE	NUMBER OF DOCUMENTS	CONTENT	STUDENT ACTIVITIES	NUMBER OF CLASS PERIODS
7. Soviet Espionage and an Atmosphere of Distrust Documents 22-25 Sound recordings D and F Worksheet 6	4	The postwar Communist scare	Evaluating a hypothesis Simulating a trial and deciding on a verdict Interpreting a graph Interpreting a sound recording	3-4
8. The Korean War Documents 26-28 Sound recording G Worksheet 7	3	The Korean War	Establishing a chronology of events Interpreting a sound recording Developing a plan based on research Evaluating the historical accuracy of a fictional account of an event	1-3
9. Harry S. Truman Documents 29-31 Worksheet 8	3	The election of 1948 Assassination attempt on Truman	Interpreting a cartoon Researching related topics	1
10. Civil Rights Documents 32-35 Worksheet 9	4	Postwar desegregation Minority postwar economic status	Identifying point of view Role-playing Developing a graph from data	2-3
11. Life in Postwar America: A Photographic Study Documents 36-40 Photograph Analysis worksheet Worksheet 10	5	Postwar changes in American life	Analyzing photographs and coming to conclusions Writing a letter	1-2

Introductory Exercises

These exercises introduce students to the general objectives of the unit. They focus students' attention on documents and their importance to the historian, who interprets and records the past. They serve as valuable opening exercises for this unit.

The Historian's Tools

The Historian's Tools worksheet is designed to increase students' awareness of the process of analyzing historical information. It focuses on both the nature of the process of analyzing historical information and those factors that influence the historian's analysis of evidence. The worksheet includes specific questions on distinctions between primary and secondary sources, the reliability of those sources, and the influence of bias, point of view, and perspective on the historian's interpretation.

Students do not analyze documents to complete this worksheet as they do in other exercises in the unit. Class discussion, however, is essential to helping students understand the issues raised by the worksheet because there are many ways to answer the questions. You may wish to assign the worksheet as homework and discuss it with students in class.

Written Document Analysis

The Written Document Analysis worksheet helps students to analyze systematically any written document in this unit. In sections 1-5 of the worksheet, students locate basic details within the document. In section 6 students analyze the document more critically as they complete items A-E. There are many possible correct answers to section 6, A-E. We suggest you use either document 2, 8, 22, or 27 with this worksheet.

Photograph Analysis

The Photograph Analysis worksheet helps students to identify systematically the historical evidence within photographs. It is designed to improve students' ability to use photographs as historical documents. It can be used specifically with exercises 1, 9, and 11.

Sound Recording Analysis

The Sound Recording Analysis worksheet helps students to identify systematically the historical evidence within recordings. It is designed to improve students' ability to listen to sound recordings as primary sources of historical information. It can be used specifically with exercises 2, 3, 5, 7, and 8.

Cartoon Analysis

The Cartoon Analysis worksheet helps students to analyze systematically any cartoon in this unit. It is designed to improve students' ability to analyze the visual and written information contained in political cartoons. It can be used specifically with exercises 4, 5, 7, and 9.

The Historian's Tools

Worksheet

1. If you were writing a chapter in your textbook on the period following World War II, list three things you would like to know about that period.

   1. _____

   2. _____

   3. _____

2. Where might you look to find information about the three topics you listed in #1?

   Topic   **Source of Information**

   _____   _____

   _____   _____

   _____   _____

3. Historians classify sources of information as **PRIMARY** or **SECONDARY**. Primary sources are those created by people who actually saw or participated in an event and recorded that event or their reactions to it immediately afterwards. Secondary sources are those created by someone either not present when that event occurred or removed from it by time. Classify the sources of information you listed in #2 as either primary or secondary by placing a **P** or **S** next to your answers in #2. Reconsider the sources you would use to find information about the postwar period; list three more here.

   1. _____

   2. _____

   3. _____

4. Some sources of historical information are viewed as more **RELIABLE** than others, though all of them may be useful. Factors such as bias, self interest, distance, and faulty memory affect the reliability of a source. Below is a list of sources of information on the 187th Regimental Combat Team's airborne assault on Munsan-ni, North Korea, in October 1950. Rate the reliability of each source on a numerical scale in which 1 is reliable and 5 very unreliable. Be able to support your ratings.

   A. A headquarters' plan for the conduct of the assault.   1   2   3   4   5

   B. A combat recording by a reporter accompanying
      the airborne assault team in combat.   1   2   3   4   5

C. A newspaper article written the day
after the assault on Munsan-ni.   1   2   3   4   5

D. A transcript of an interview conducted with an
eyewitness 8 years after the assault on Munsan-ni.   1   2   3   4   5

E. A U.S. history high-school textbook
description of the Korean war.   1   2   3   4   5

F. A description of the Korean war in an encyclopedia. 1   2   3   4   5

5. What personal and social factors might influence historians as they write about people and events of the past?

_____

_____

_____

6. What personal and social factors influence *you* as you read historical accounts of people and events?

_____

_____

_____

Designed and developed by the education staff of the National Archives and Records Administration, Washington, DC 20408.

Written Document Analysis

Worksheet

1. Type of Document (Check one):
    _____ Newspaper   _____ Map   _____ Advertisement
    _____ Letter   _____ Telegram   _____ Congressional record
    _____ Patent   _____ Press release   _____ Census report
    _____ Memorandum   _____ Report   _____ Other

2. Unique Physical Qualities of the Document (check one or more):
    _____ Interesting letterhead   _____ Notations
    _____ Handwritten   _____ "RECEIVED" stamp
    _____ Typed   _____ Other
    _____ Seals

3. Date(s) of Document: _____

4. Author (or creator) of the Document: _____

    Position (Title): _____

5. For What Audience was the Document Written? _____

6. Document Information (There are many possible ways to answer A-E.)

    A. List three things the author said that you think are important:

        1. _____

        2. _____

        3. _____

    B. Why do you think this document was written?

        _____

        _____

    C. What evidence in the document helps you to know why it was written?
        Quote from the document.

        _____

        _____

    D. List two things the document tells you about life in the United States
        at the time it was written:

        1. _____

        2. _____

    E. Write a question to the author that is left unanswered by the document:

        _____

        _____

Designed and developed by the education staff of the National Archives and Records Administration, Washington, DC 20408.

Photograph Analysis

Worksheet

Step 1. Observation

A. Study the photograph for 2 minutes. Form an overall impression of the photograph and then examine individual items. Next, divide the photo into quadrants and study each section to see what new details become visible.

B. Use the chart below to list people, objects, and activities in the photograph.

PEOPLE	OBJECTS	ACTIVITIES
_____	_____	_____
_____	_____	_____
_____	_____	_____
_____	_____	_____
_____	_____	_____
_____	_____	_____

Step 2. Inference

Based on what you have observed above, list three things you might infer from this photograph:

1. _____

2. _____

3. _____

Step 3. Questions

A. What questions does this photograph raise in your mind?

_____

_____

B. Where could you find answers to them?

_____

_____

Designed and developed by the education staff of the National Archives and Records Administration, Washington, DC 20408.

Sound Recording Analysis

Worksheet

Step 1. Pre-listening

A. Whose voices will you hear on this recording? _____

_____

B. What is the date of this recording? _____

C. Where was this recording made? _____

Step 2. Listening

A. Type of sound recording (check one):

_____ Policy speech   _____Congressional testimony

_____ News report   _____Interview

_____ Entertainment broadcast   _____Press conference

_____ Convention proceedings   _____Campaign speech

_____ Arguments before a court   _____Other

_____ Panel discussion

B. Unique physical qualities of the recording

_____ Music   _____Special sound effects

_____ Live broadcast   _____Background sound

_____ Narrated

C. What is the tone or mood of this sound recording?_____

_____

Step 3. Post-listening (or repeated listening)

A. List three things in this sound recording that you think are important:

1. _____

2. _____

3. _____

B. Why do you think the original broadcast was made and for what audience?

_____

_____

C. What evidence in the recording helps you to know why it was made?

_____

_____

D. List two things this sound recording tells you about life in the United States at the time it was made:

1. _____

2. _____

E. Write a question to the broadcaster that is left unanswered by this sound recording:

_____

_____

F. What information do you gain about this event that would not be conveyed by a written transcript? Be specific.

_____

_____

Designed and developed by the education staff of the National Archives and Records Administration, Washington, DC 20408.

Cartoon Analysis

Worksheet

Visuals	Words (not all cartoons include words)
Step One 1. List the objects or people you see in the cartoon.	1. Identify the cartoon caption and/or title. 2. Locate three words or phrases used by the cartoonist to identify objects or people within the cartoon. 3. Record any important dates or numbers that appear in the cartoon.
Step Two 2. Which of the objects on your list are symbols? 3. What do you think each symbol means?	4. Which words or phrases in the cartoon appear to be the most significant? Why do you think so? 5. List adjectives that describe the emotions portrayed in the cartoon.

Step Three

A.   Describe the action taking place in the cartoon.

B.   Explain how the words in the cartoon clarify the symbols.

C.   Explain the message of the cartoon.

D.   What special interest groups would agree/disagree with the cartoon's message? Why?

Designed and developed by the education staff of the National Archives and Records Administration, Washington, DC 20408.

Exercise 1
The Beginning of the Atomic Age

Note to the Teacher:

Following the death of President Franklin D. Roosevelt in April 1945, Secretary of War Stimson informed the newly sworn-in President, Harry S. Truman, about the Manhattan Engineer District project. At four major sites, research and production of necessary components was advancing the creation of the atomic bomb. J. Robert Oppenheimer, head of the bomb development laboratory at Los Alamos, NM, indicated to the project supervisor, Maj. Gen. Leslie Groves, that the bomb was ready to be tested by mid-July. The scientists of Los Alamos were uncertain of the power of the weapon they had developed. Some thought it would not work; others feared that it might ignite the Earth's atmosphere. To be safe, Oppenheimer filed plans with the office of the Governor of New Mexico to evacuate the state. At 5:30 a.m. on July 16, the first atomic bomb was exploded at Alamogordo, NM. **Document 1** consists of the notes and sketches of the July 16th "Trinity" blast that Luis W. Alvarez, a project scientist, made from an airplane.

On July 26 Allied leaders meeting in Potsdam, Germany, issued an ultimatum demanding the unconditional surrender of the Empire of Japan. Following the rejection of the ultimatum by Japanese military leaders, President Truman authorized the dropping of the atomic bomb. Hiroshima was bombed on August 6 and Nagasaki on August 9. At the insistence of Emperor Hirohito, Japan surrendered on August 14. The United States had been prepared to drop a third bomb, as indicated in **document 2**, if Japan had not surrendered.

The monopoly of the United States in atomic weaponry ended on September 23, 1949, when President Truman announced that the Soviet Union had successfully tested an atomic bomb. In January 1950 Truman notified the U.S. public that the United States was developing a more powerful weapon, the hydrogen bomb. Manufacture of the hydrogen bomb began in 1952, but by 1953 the Soviets had developed their own hydrogen bomb. The arms race prompted a renewal in civil defense preparations. **Document 3** shows students ducking under their desks and covering their heads as part of a school bomb drill.

For an explanation of the content of **document 13**, see exercise 4.

Time: 2 to 3 class periods

Objectives:

- To analyze a photograph for information.

- To compare and contrast civil defense measures of the 1950s and the present.

- To conduct research into types of school and local civil defense resources.

Materials Needed:

Documents 1-3 and 13
Photograph Analysis worksheet, p. 14

Procedures:

1. Duplicate and distribute documents 1-3 and ask students to examine them closely. Ask students to share their initial reaction to the documents. Ask students to select one of the following roles and write a paragraph reacting to information found in the related document.

    a. As if you were an observer of the "Trinity" blast, write a description of it.

    b. As if you were President Truman, write a note denying authorization to use the third bomb.

    c. As if you were one of the students in the photograph, write a monologue telling what would be going through your mind when the photograph was taken.

2. Duplicate and distribute the Photograph Analysis worksheet and ask students to use it to analyze document 3.

3. Direct students to gather information that will help them compare their community's civil defense plans in the period 1948-53 with those of today, noting ways these plans are similar and ways they are different. Students should then organize their findings into handouts that could be distributed at school.

4. Extended activity: Arrange for a civil defense representative to serve as a guest speaker to your class.

Exercise 2

The Conversion from War to Peace

Note to the Teacher:

Following V-J Day, Americans eagerly began to convert swords into ploughshares. A number of war-related matters demanded attention, however. The broken Axis nations of Germany and Japan were occupied by the Allies. Germany was divided into sectors administered by the United States, Great Britain, France, and the Soviet Union. Although Japan was nominally administered by a joint Allied commission, the United States took major responsibility for its occupation. In both cases the Allies demilitarized the occupied nations, dismantled their totalitarian regimes, and, in Japan and West Germany, introduced democratic principles and forms of government.

The Allied nations held war crimes trials in both Germany and Japan. Although the Nuremberg trials are better known, Japanese war crimes trials were held from January 1946 to November 1948. Seven top civilian and military leaders, including Premier Tojo, were executed. A special tribunal for military offenses operated until late 1949, convicting 4,200 Japanese soldiers of atrocities and executing 720 for war crimes. **Document 4** is a U.S. military memo regarding Soviet interrogation of Japanese generals awaiting trial in 1947. U.S. occupation of Japan ended 4 years later, on September 8, 1951, with the ratification of a peace treaty between the United States and Japan.

For most Americans, the conversion from war to peace took place on a personal level, whether it was a returning G.I. or a family coping with the upheaval in economic conditions. Inflation was a primary concern. Many price and rationing controls imposed by the Office of Price Administration (OPA) during the war ended by November 1946. Fearful that the end of wartime programs would lead to shortages and inflation, consumers and labor supported extending the OPA, which had set maximum prices for commodities and rents (**sound recording A**), while business argued for removing the regulations of OPA. The OPA was terminated in 1947.

Prices rose immediately, but wage increases lagged behind the inflation rate, creating labor unrest and strikes. Republicans, elected to a majority in Congress in 1946, responded to the unrest with new labor legislation. **Document 5** is a letter to Truman from American Federation of Labor President William Green opposing the Taft-Hartley Act, which had been approved by Congress, and urging the President to veto the bill. Although Truman vetoed the bill in June 1947, Congress overturned his veto, and the Taft-Hartley Act became law. Its effect was to curtail gains made by labor during the New Deal.

One of the most significant reconversion measures was the Serviceman's Readjustment Act of 1944. This act, informally known as the G.I. Bill, provided medical, educational, and housing benefits to veterans of World War II. By the end of 1952, 10 million veterans had received $13.5 billion in subsistence allowance and fees for school supplies and tuition. **Document 6** is a pamphlet produced in 1947 by the American Veterans Committee at the University of Michigan. It reported that surveyed student veterans supported an increase in the subsistence allotment. The G.I. Bill programs for World War II veterans lasted until 1956.

Time: 1 to 2 class periods

Objectives:

- To examine and evaluate the impact of postwar domestic legislation.

- To compare and contrast domestic legislation following World War II with that following World War I.

- To examine issues emerging from the war crimes trials.

- To interpret information from a graph.

Materials Needed:

Documents 4-6
Sound recording A
Worksheet 1

Procedures:

1. Duplicate documents 5 and 6 and worksheet 1. After students have completed the assignment, answer questions they might have.

2. Divide the class into six groups and hand out copies of documents 5 and 6 to each group. Instruct students to examine the documents and carefully listen to sound recording A in order to answer the following questions:

    a. What government action is the subject of each document?

    b. What will be the effect of the action from the point of view of the originators of each document?

    c. What action does the originator of each document want the government to take?

    Ask each group to research in textbooks and/ or the school library the following questions:

    d. What action did the government take in each of these instances and what effect did it have?

    e. What are the differences and similarities between government legislation on wages and price controls, labor relations, and educational benefits following World War I and following World War II?

    f. What wage and price controls have been imposed since World War II?

    g. What major changes have been made in labor law since the Taft-Hartley Act?

    h. What educational benefits did veterans of Korea and Vietnam receive?

3. Duplicate and distribute document 4 and ask students to read the document carefully. Ask them to note that the memo defines limits for Soviet interrogation of Japanese generals held for the war crime of engaging in biological warfare research on Chinese prisoners of war. Discuss as a class the following questions:

    a. What protections should international law afford prisoners of war?

    b. Where does "obeying orders" end and personal responsibility begin for the soldier in times of war?

c. Can defeated enemies receive a fair trial from victors?

d. How do nations that are unfriendly maintain a working relationship?

e. Because great attention has been placed on nuclear warfare and there is an active nuclear freeze movement, much less is said about the chemical and biological weapons and tactics of conventional warfare. Examine whether these weapons are necessary and ethical. Should we or should we not consider whether the use of certain weapons is ethical?

Worksheet 1 answers: 1. married without kids 2. married with kids 3. $58.25 4. answers will vary 5. withdrawing savings 6. 69% 7. 18% 8. 65% 9. $125 or more and $15 or more per child 10. no, answers will vary

THE TRUMAN YEARS: 1945-1953

Exercise 2: The Conversion from War to Peace

Worksheet 1

Directions: Use information from document 6 to complete the worksheet.

WHERE DOES THE MONEY GO?

1. Which group of students requires the most money to live?

   _____

2. Which group of students spends the most money on food?

   _____

3. How much money does the unmarried student spend on the category that includes clothing, insurance, laundry, cleaning, transportation, etc.?

   _____

4. How do you account for the fact that married students without children spend more money than other students?

   _____

   _____

FROM WHAT SOURCES DO THEY MAKE UP THE DEFICIT?

5. What is the most common way of making up average monthly living costs?

   _____

6. Look at the percentage of married students without children who depend on the wife's employment and the percentage of married students with children who depend on the wife's employment. What is the difference in the percentages?

   _____

   _____

WHAT DO STUDENT VETS WANT?

7. What percentage of unmarried students wants an adjustment of $100?

   _____

8. What percentage of married students wants an adjustment of over $120?

   _____

9. What adjustments do most married students with children want?

   _____

10. Do we know how many student veterans participated in this survey? How does that affect the validity and value of this report?

    _____

    _____

Exercise 3
Cold War and Containment

Note to the Teacher:

Less than a year after V-E Day, the successful wartime alliance of the United States, Great Britain, and the Soviet Union had deteriorated. In February 1946 George F. Kennan, one of the nation's foremost experts on Russia and chargé d'affaires at the U.S. Embassy in the Soviet Union, telegrammed the Secretary of State and warned him of Soviet expansionism. A few weeks later, in a speech at Westminister College in Fulton, MO, Winston Churchill proclaimed that an "iron curtain" had descended over Eastern Europe and warned Americans that tyranny imperiled Western Europe (**sound recording B**). He urged the formation of an Anglo-American military alliance to deter Soviet aggression.

As Soviet pressure increased in Europe, Iran, and China, the United States responded by implementing a policy of containment through military and economic aid and alliances. In March 1947 President Truman requested $400 million in aid to Greece and Turkey (**sound recording C**). The Truman Doctrine, as this plan came to be known, was approved by Congress in the hope of preventing the further spread of communism. In February 1948, however, Communists staged a coup in Czechoslovakia. Western leaders resolved to respond firmly to avoid any repetition of appeasement over Czechoslovakia, such as that which had contributed to the outbreak of World War II. On June 11 the Senate adopted a resolution sponsored by Michigan's Republican Senator Arthur H. Vandenberg that supported U.S. association in regional collective security arrangements permitted under the U.N. Charter. This resolution paved the way for the U.S. role in establishing the North Atlantic Treaty Organization.

Thirteen days later the Communists blockaded land routes to the military occupation zones of Berlin administered by Great Britain, France, and the United States. The Americans did not want to abandon Berlin, but neither did they want to provoke a third world war by confronting the Soviets and East Germans with armed convoys. The dilemma was solved by Gen. Lucius Clay, who suggested an airlift. From June 26, 1948, to May 12, 1949, 2,100,000 West Berliners and Western military forces were supplied by the airborne lifeline (**document 7**). The Berlin blockade intensified Western European and U.S. efforts to form a North Atlantic defensive alliance, and on April 4, 1949, the North Atlantic Treaty was signed. It was submitted to the Senate for approval. The opposition of influential Republican Senator Robert A. Taft of Ohio (**document 8**) was countered by fellow Republican Arthur Vandenberg, who urged ratification because the treaty "spells out the conclusive warning that independent freedom is not an orphan in the western world, and that no armed aggression will have a chance to win...." The Senate consented to the treaty in July by a vote of 82-13.

Communist expansion was checked in Europe, but not in China. Since 1946, civil war had raged between the Nationalist Chinese, led by Chiang Kaishek, and the Chinese Communists, led by Mao Tse-tung. In early 1947 the United States abandoned mediation efforts, condemning both sides for their lack of good faith. By late 1949, with the Nationalists' cause apparently doomed, U.S. policymakers considered ways of standing clear of Chiang while leaving open the possibility of establishing relations with the newly proclaimed People's Republic of China (PRC). **Documents 9** and **10** are letters to Secretary of State Dean Acheson, the first from Senator Edwin C. Johnson of Colorado, urging recognition of the PRC, the second from Senator H. Alexander Smith of New Jersey, opposing recognition of the PRC. Shortly thereafter Mao challenged the Nationalists' representation of China in the United Nations. On December 8, 1949, Chiang Kai-shek and his Nationalist followers abandoned mainland China and moved to the island of Formosa (Taiwan), where they set up a government called the Republic of China (Nationalist China).

The United States moved to contain communism in the underdeveloped countries of the world, especially in Latin America and Africa. The fourth point in Truman's 1949 inaugural address was a proposal for "a bold new program for making the benefits of our scientific advances and industrial progress available for the improvement and growth of underdeveloped areas." Although the Point Four program was never fully funded, by 1952 U.S. advisors were present in 33 nations, providing technical assistance in essential fields of economic activity (**document 11**).

The struggle for the minds of the nonaligned people of the world is demonstrated in **document 12**, Senate Resolution 243, which called for a "Marshall plan in the field of ideas" for the propagation of the democratic creed.

Time: 2 to 4 class periods

Objectives:

- To describe the policy of containment and the means by which the policy was carried out.

- To examine considerations taken in formulating U.S. foreign policy in China.

- To identify point of view in primary sources.

Materials Needed:

Documents 7-12
Sound recordings B and C
Worksheet 2

Procedures:

Note: Before beginning the procedures, you may want to use the Sound Recording Analysis worksheet, p. 15, with the sound recordings if your students are unfamiliar with gathering data from sound recordings.

1. Duplicate and distribute worksheet 2 to each student. Play sound recordings B and C to the entire class, then duplicate and distribute a set of documents 7-12 to groups of 2-3 students. After students complete the worksheet, review it and discuss any questions your students may raise.

2. Either make a transparency of document 11 or list its "Essential Fields of Economic Activity" on the chalkboard. Ask the students to judge which fields now seem obsolete and which fields they would expect to include in such a list today. As a group, brainstorm a list of essential fields of economic activity for the present. Ask each student to make a list predicting the essential fields of economic activity 30 years from now. Ask them to review their lists of predictions to see if their anticipated future careers are related to any of these fields.

3

3. Duplicate and distribute copies of documents 9 and 10 to each student. Draw the students' attention to the legislators who served on the senators' committees. Ask students to identify the positions of Senator Johnson and Senator Alexander on the issue of recognizing the People's Republic of China. Once they have identified the positions, instruct them to outline the supporting reasons presented by the senators for their respective opinions. Ask students to write a paragraph identifying which document was the more persuasive and giving reasons that support their opinions. If time permits ask several students to research and share with the class the policy adopted by Truman toward China and the evolution of that policy from 1947 to the present.

4. As a class, come to an agreement on a definition of "containment." Divide the class into groups and ask students to review postwar containment programs, then decide whether they are a continuation of, or a departure from, previous U.S. foreign policies. Ask each group to evaluate containment in relation to one of the following:

   a. Washington's Farewell Address

   b. The Monroe Doctrine

   c. Wilson's Missionary Diplomacy in Latin American affairs and in the Treaty of Versailles

   d. Rejection of the Covenant of the League of Nations

   e. Armed Neutrality (WW II)

   f. Ratification of the United Nations Charter

5. Instruct students to assume the role of a Soviet reporter for *Pravda* during the Truman years. Ask students to write an editorial about the U.S. policy of containment from the Soviet perspective.

Exercise 3: Cold War and Containment

Worksheet 2

Directions: Listen to sound recordings B and C and study documents 7-12 to complete the chart.

	What ideas of the cold war are expressed in this source?	How is the policy of containment advanced in this document?
Sound recording B		
Sound recording C		
Doc. 7		
Doc. 8		
Doc. 9		
Doc. 10		
Doc. 11		
Doc. 12		

Exercise 4
Civilian Control of the Military

Note to the Teacher:

The principle of civilian supremacy over the military is embodied in the Constitution. During the postwar era, elected authorities reasserted their right to make some policy decisions that had often been yielded to the military during World War II.

Throughout World War II, research in atomic energy had focused on military applications and had been directed by military authorities. With the surrender of Japan, although atomic power was still primarily researched for potential weaponry, there was increasing interest in possible peaceful uses of the new energy source. In December 1945 Senator Brien McMahon of Connecticut introduced legislation to enable private entrepreneurs to develop peacetime applications of atomic power under the auspices of an Atomic Energy Commission, which would supervise the government's monopoly of radioactive materials and atomic processes and facilities. Secretary of War Patterson opposed the McMahon bill. He viewed the power of the atom as a military force and feared that national security would be compromised if atomic technology fell into civilian hands. The original bill was amended so that a military liaison board would advise the Atomic Energy Commission of its concerns, but disputes between the board and the commission would be settled by the President. On August 1, 1946, President Truman signed the bill into law. **Document 13** is a press release announcing the transfer of the atomic energy program from the Department of War to the U.S. Atomic Energy Commission and reaffirming the principle of civilian supremacy.

During World War II, it became apparent that the independence of each branch of the armed forces from the other branches was inefficient. In the summer of 1945, the idea of unifying the army and navy began to gain force. In December, in a message to Congress, President Truman called for a reorganization of the armed forces. In May 1946 Truman called upon the Secretaries of the Army and the Navy to work out a plan. By the end of the month, areas of agreement were decided upon, as were areas of continued disagreement. The President reviewed the plan and decided on matters unresolved by the army and navy. Finally, on January 16, 1947, acceptance by all parties of a compromise unification plan was announced. **Document 14**, the cartoon titled "Everything Unified, Everybody Happy," was a response to the announcement. A month later the compromise plan was submitted to the House of Representatives; on July 25, 1947, the National Security Act became law. It provided for the coordination of the army, navy, and air force into the single National Military Establishment under the civilian Secretary of Defense. It also established the Joint Chiefs of Staff, the Central Intelligence Agency, and the National Security Council. In 1949 the act was amended and the National Military Establishment was renamed the Department of Defense.

The most celebrated confrontation between civilian and military authority occurred during the Korean war between President Truman and Gen. Douglas MacArthur. Throughout the winter of 1951, MacArthur had criticized the U.S. policy of limited warfare, which gave "privileged sanctuary" to Chinese bases in Manchuria. On March 25, in violation of a December 1950 order to clear all public statements through the White House, MacArthur threatened publicly to send naval and air forces to attack China if the enemy did not surrender. His speech undermined quiet efforts to negotiate an armistice. (See exercise 8, **document 28**.) MacArthur reiterated this position in a letter to Representative Joseph Martin of Massachusetts, the leader of the Republicans in the House, who released it to the newspapers in early April. Truman believed that MacArthur's insubordination would lead the United States into a third world war. He had insisted on a policy of limited warfare because the United Nations mandate was to preserve the integrity of the Republic of Korea rather than to achieve total victory. Truman feared that a general war in Asia might divert U.S. strength; lead to Communist attacks in Western Europe, Okinawa, and Japan; and escalate into a nuclear war. As a result, on April 11 President Truman fired MacArthur **(document 15)**. Public reaction to Truman's actions was swift and unfavorable, as **document 16** illustrates. Truman defended his decision by explaining that MacArthur's actions had thwarted the policies developed by elected political officials and were subversive of the constitutional principle of civilian primacy over the military. In addition, as Chairman of the Joint Chiefs of Staff Omar Bradley stated, it would be "the wrong war, at the wrong place, at the wrong time, and with the wrong enemy."

Some historians now believe that the real issue was the appropriate way to fight the Korean war. The controversy went to the heart of Truman's cold war strategy in general (Europe-oriented) and his handling of the Korean war in particular (limited war). In the latter instance, for example, MacArthur argued correctly that the administration had been inconsistent in its Korean war objectives. At first Truman had wanted just to defend South Korea, but after the victory at Inchon, he tried to liberate the entire peninsula. Then, when the Chinese entered the war, Truman switched back to being satisfied with just defending South Korea.

Time: 2 to 3 class periods

Objectives:

- To read for facts and general content.

- To examine the relationship between civil and military authorities under the Constitution.

- To identify and evaluate arguments and to formulate a position on an issue.

- To identify and interpret visual and written symbols in a political cartoon.

Materials needed:

Documents 13-16
Worksheet 3

Procedures:

1. Duplicate and distribute document 13 and worksheet 3 and ask students to examine the document and complete the worksheet.

2. Duplicate and distribute documents 14-16 and ask students to read them. If they have not already examined the cartoons, you may wish to have the students analyze them using the Cartoon Analysis worksheet on page 17. If students have difficulty translating the telegram, explain to them that punctuation is either spelled out or abbreviated (PD for period, PARA for paragraph, CMA for comma, and SUGAR for the letter "s").

3. Divide the class into four groups.

    a. Assign one of the following issues to each group.

    b. Direct students to list arguments for both sides of the issue they are examining. Tell them to choose a spokesperson.

    c. After 20-30 minutes, ask that speaker to state the issue and discuss the arguments with the class.

4

d. Ask students to select one of the issues and write a short paper in which they formulate a position on the issue, including at least three supporting pieces of evidence.

The issues are as follows:

- Should military commanders be permitted to publicize their disagreements with war policies of elected officials? Under what circumstances does free speech for military officials end and insubordination begin?

- President Truman wrote in his memoirs, "It is a mistake to believe only the military can safeguard national security . . . preservation of the nation's safety and defense is an organic and sweeping responsibility that extends to all branches and departments of the government." Cite events that support or refute Truman's assertion.

- U.S. tradition and statutory provisions prohibit active armed forces personnel from serving in other government posts. What are the arguments for and against this prohibition?

- Should war policy be determined by a civilian government or by the military command at the front lines? What are the strengths and weaknesses of each approach? What does the Constitution say about the issue of civil/ military relations?

Everything Unified, Everybody Happy

Exercise 4: Civilian Control of the Military

Worksheet 3

Directions: Use information from document 13 and your own opinions to complete the worksheet.

1. What is the main idea of this document?

   _____

   _____

2. What people in the past recognized the need for the creation of the Atomic Energy Commission?

   _____

   _____

3. What person in this document is recognized for his achievements?

   _____

   _____

4. Why might it be important for Secretary of War Patterson to pledge the cooperation and support of the War Department?

   _____

   _____

5. In your opinion, how did the transfer of the atomic energy program from the military to a civilian commission affect applications of atomic power?

   _____

   _____

6. Is government monopoly of materials, facilities, and processes of nuclear energy an appropriate and efficient way to handle development of nuclear power?

   _____

   _____

Exercise 5
The Marshall Plan

Note to the Teacher:

In the spring of 1947, after the end of the most destructive war in human history, most of the countries of Europe were on the verge of economic collapse. The meager assistance provided to Western Europe by UNRRA (United Nations Relief and Rehabilitation Administration) was ending before industrial and agricultural recovery had begun. U.S. administration officials feared that Western Europe would fall under the Soviet sphere of influence if the United States did not provide aid.

On June 5, 1947, Secretary of State George C. Marshall proposed a European recovery program in a commencement address at Harvard University (**sound recording E**). The foreign ministers of Great Britain, France, and the Soviet Union met from June 27 to July 2 to consider Marshall's proposal. Although the Soviets and their Eastern European satellites refused to participate in the plan, 16 countries accepted the idea and met on July 12 to establish a Committee for European Economic Cooperation, whose purpose was to estimate the aid necessary to reconstruct Western Europe's economy and to begin cooperative economic planning. The Committee's report in September asserted that Western Europe would need 16.4 to 22.4 billion dollars over the next 4 years.

On December 19, President Truman responded by sending a $17 billion European Recovery Plan to Congress. Senate bill 2202 (**document 17**) was introduced in January 1948, but met with some opposition by resurgent isolationists. On February 28, Communists overthrew the government of Czechoslovakia. Responding quickly, Congress adopted the bill and Truman signed it into law on April 3. The European Recovery Act provided $5.3 billion in aid during its first 12 months and a total of $13 billion from 1948 to 1952. **Document 18**, a cartoon from the *Tampa Tribune* of April 10, 1949, expresses confidence in the program's effectiveness a year after it was enacted. At the end of 4 years of Marshall Plan assistance, the participating nations exceeded their prewar production levels by an average of 40 percent.

Time: 1 class period

Objectives:

- To identify the reasons for and effects of the Marshall Plan and relate the plan to the policy of containment.

- To listen to a historical recording, identify significant information, and describe the tone or mood of the recording.

- To identify and interpret visual and written symbols in a political cartoon.

Materials Needed:

Documents 17 and 18
Sound recording E
Sound Recording Analysis worksheet, p. 15
Worksheet 4

Procedures:

1. Duplicate and distribute the Sound Recording Analysis worksheet to students. Before playing the sound recording, share information from the Note to the Teacher to enable students to fill out part A. Play the segment called the "Marshall Plan" speech and ask students to complete the part B questions as they listen to the speech. After students have listened to the speech, allow them time to answer part C, then review the worksheet and discuss any questions your students may raise. Ask them to speculate on the reactions of the United States, western Europe, and the Soviet Union to the speech.

2. Duplicate documents 17 and 18 and worksheet 4, give a copy to each student, and direct students to complete the chart. Replay the sound recording of the Marshall Plan speech to assist students in completing that section of the worksheet.

3. Ask students to review document 17 and to notice how the bill creating the Marshall Plan both builds a rationale for the bill and explains how it will work. You may use the following questions as a guide for discussion.

    a. According to the writers of this legislation, what are the results of the existing situation in Europe?

    b. What conditions do they assert are necessary for the principles of individual liberty, free institutions, and genuine independence to flourish?

    c. According to the writers, what steps should the plan of economic recovery follow in order to accomplish its objectives?

4. Lead the students in a discussion about why the United States decided to extend aid to the Europeans. Then ask them to write a paragraph in answer to the question: Why is foreign aid being extended to countries around the world today?

Exercise 5: The Marshall Plan

Worksheet 4

Directions: Complete the chart.

	Sound recording E	Document 17	Document 18
What type of document is this?		An act by both houses of Congress	
When was this document made?	June 5, 1947		
What does this document tell about the Marshall Plan?	Purpose to restore European economy. Europeans determine needs, Americans provide aid.		
How does this document reflect the principle of containment?			Marshall Plan contains Soviet threats, sabotage.
How does this document show application of the principle of self-determination?		Restoration of healthy economy will restore or maintain genuine independence.	
Who is the intended audience of this document?			Readers of the *Tampa Tribune*

Exercise 6
Israel and the Middle East

Note to the Teacher:

At the conclusion of World War I, the Ottoman Empire was broken up and its Middle Eastern states were assigned by the League of Nations to European powers. Great Britain received the mandate over Palestine, a country that contained both Arab and Jewish populations that were strongly nationalistic. Britain angered the Arab population when it promised to establish a Jewish "national home" within the borders of Palestine. The admission of large numbers of Jewish immigrants before and after World War II further fueled violent Arab reaction to British administration.

The British in 1947, caught between Arab nationalism and Jewish insistence that a Palestinian homeland be created to prevent future holocausts, turned to the United Nations for help. On November 29, the U.N. General Assembly adopted a resolution recommending the partition of Palestine into an Arab state and a Jewish state. The holy city of Jerusalem would be internationalized and administered by the United Nations. The resolution, although accepted by the Jews, was rejected by the Arabs. On May 14, 1948, the British mandate expired and Britain withdrew its troops. Simultaneously, the United Nations proclaimed the state of Israel and the Arab states surrounding Israel declared war on the new state, launching a military offensive on several fronts. On May 15, the United States recognized the new nation of Israel, at that time under the leadership of Chaim Weizmann and David Ben-Gurion (**document 19**).

Israel's military situation was desperate as the new state struggled to repel attacks from Egypt, Syria, Lebanon, Transjordan (modern Jordan), Iraq, Saudi Arabia, and Yemen as well as internal attacks by Palestinian Arabs. **Document 20** is a map of Israel's military situation on June 11, 1948. Israeli resistance preserved the new state. The United Nations attempted to negotiate a settlement to the war, but, on September 17, U.N. mediator Count Folke Bernadotte of Sweden was assassinated in Jerusalem. His successor was Dr. Ralph J. Bunche, a black diplomat from the United States. In March 1949, terms of an armistice developed by Bunche were accepted by both Arabs and Israelis (**document 21**). Unfortunately, the armistice did not solve the underlying bitterness between the two groups. Palestinians refused to live under Israeli rule, and 600,000 Palestinians moved into refugee camps in neighboring Arab states. These Arab states refused to recognize Israel's right to exist.

Because the United States recognized Israel, U.S. relations with Arab states were strained, opening opportunities for the Soviets to expand their influence in this strategic region. Dr. Bunche's peacemaking efforts, however, earned him the 1950 Nobel Peace Prize.

Time: 1 to 2 class periods

Objectives:

- To interpret information from a map.

- To describe U.S. policies in the Middle East following World War II.

Materials Needed:

Documents 19-21
Worksheet 5

6 Procedures:

1. Duplicate document 20 and worksheet 5 and distribute copies to each student. After pupils have completed questions 1-5, discuss the worksheet as a class.

   If possible, locate maps of Israel that reflect changes because of Arab-Israeli conflicts in 1956, 1967, and 1973; the Camp David accords in 1979; and the most recent peace talks. Permit students time to study the maps and instruct them to complete the last question on the worksheet.

2. Duplicate documents 19 and 21 and distribute copies to students. Ask pupils to fit them into the chronology of postwar U.S. diplomatic relations in the Middle East.

   a. Pose to the students the question: What conditions might have accounted for the speed of U.S. recognition of Israel?

   b. Direct students to search a library for information necessary to create a time line of significant events in the U.S. Middle East policy from 1947 to the present.

3. Extended activities: Students may wish to select one of the following assignments to understand more clearly the relations among the United States, Israel, and the Arab states. Ask them to share their findings through oral presentations with the class.

   a. Read either a nonfictional work, such as *Oh, Jerusalem* by Collins and LaPierre, or a fictional work, such as *Exodus* by Leon Uris, that describes the issues, emotions, and events surrounding the formation of the state of Israel. Formulate answers to these questions:

      • How do these descriptions accord with the historical information?

      • How do these descriptions enlarge one's sense of the events?

      • Do these descriptions alter your sense of the historical information? If so, in what ways?

   b. Research U.S. policy on diplomatic relations with other countries.

      Determine answers to the following questions:

      • How does the U.S. government decide to recognize a country?

      • What are the mechanics of recognizing a country and how long does it ordinarily take?

      • How is an embassy established?

      • What responsibilities does a U.S. embassy have?

      • How does the United States deal with nations that do not have full diplomatic relations with the United States?

   c. Collect biographical information about Dr. Ralph Bunche. What other citizens of the United States have received the Noble Peace Prize and for what accomplishments?

Exercise 6: Israel and the Middle East

Worksheet 5

Directions: Study the map (document 20) and answer the following questions.

1. Who controls or holds the following towns?

   a. Tel Aviv _____

   b. Bethlehem _____

   c. Jericho _____

   d. Nazareth _____

   e. Jerusalem _____

2. What is the distance between the following capitals?

   a. Jerusalem and Amman _____

   b. Jerusalem and Damascus _____

   c. Jerusalem and Beirut _____

   d. Damascus and Beirut _____

3. What transportation systems are Jewish controlled or held?
   _____

4. What transportation systems are Arab controlled or held?
   _____

5. How secure are the connections between Jewish-held Jerusalem and Jewish-held coastal areas? Explain.
   _____
   _____

6. Compare and contrast document 20 with maps, if they are available, showing Israel's borders in:

   a. 1949-55 _____

   b. 1956-66 _____

   c. 1967-72 _____

   d. 1973-79 _____

   e. 1980-present _____

   What accounts for these changes? _____
   _____

Exercise 7
Soviet Espionage and an Atmosphere of Distrust

Note to the Teacher:

As the cold war intensified and Americans became troubled by a stalemate in Korea and Soviet mastery of the atomic bomb, they looked for reasons that could explain the decline in U.S. stature since V-J Day. To many people, the explanation appeared to be simple and obvious: traitors were passing secrets to the Soviets and subverting the minds of Americans. To be sure, there was reason for concern. As early as 1946, the Canadian government uncovered a Russian spy ring, and in England Klaus Fuchs was convicted for stealing atomic secrets. The U.S. press demanded investigations into the loyalty of government employees. In an attempt to rid the government of subversives, Truman issued the Loyalty Order in 1947, which authorized investigation of employees of the executive branch. At about the same time, the House Un-American Activities Committee investigated communism in the motion picture industry **(sound recording D)**. In early 1949, 11 U.S. Communist Party leaders were tried for violations of the 1940 Alien Registration Act (Smith Act). They were convicted of advocating and teaching the overthrow of the government of the United States and were sentenced to 5 years in prison.

One of the most sensational cases was that of Alger Hiss, a former upper-level official in the Department of State. In August 1948 Whittaker Chambers, a self-confessed courier for the Soviet spy network in the United States, accused Hiss of espionage and treason before the House Un-American Activities Committee **(sound recording F)**. In December, Chambers led investigators to a Maryland pumpkin patch. Microfilm that was hidden in a hollowed pumpkin, when enlarged, proved to contain secret diplomatic documents. Since the statute of limitations for espionage had run out, Hiss was indicted for perjury, was found guilty, and was sentenced to 5 years in prison.

Shortly after Hiss' sentencing, Republican Senator Joseph R. McCarthy of Wisconsin, in Wheeling, WV, on February 9, 1950, charged, "I have here in my hand a list of 205 [the number McCarthy used is disputed] — a list of names that were known to the Secretary of State as being members of the Communist Party and who nevertheless are still working and shaping the policy of the State Department." A subcommittee of the Senate Foreign Relations Committee, under the chairmanship of conservative Democrat Millard Tydings of Maryland, was appointed by the Senate to investigate McCarthy's charges. The subcommittee found the charges to be a "fraud and a hoax." McCarthy responded by attacking Tydings **(document 22)**. In the senatorial elections of 1950, McCarthy provided Tydings' opponent with a doctored photo that showed Tydings with the leader of the American Communist Party. The smear tactic undoubtedly contributed to Tydings' defeat and extended McCarthy's power.

In such a climate, if a conservative Democrat such as Tydings or a respected diplomat such as Hiss could be a "communist sympathizer" and a "fellow traveler," anyone could be "red." Even the state bird of Rhode Island, the Rhode Island Red, could be suspect, as the cartoon, "Are You a Communist?" **(document 23)** suggests.

Another sensational case involved Julius and Ethel Rosenberg. In 1951 the Rosenbergs were tried and convicted of conspiracy during and after World War II, their alleged conspiracy having consisted of transmitting to the Soviet Union information relating to U.S. national defense and the atomic bomb. The Rosenbergs were sentenced to death by electrocution. They requested stays of execution **(document 24)** while they appealed their conviction on the basis of pretrial publicity **(document 25)** and on the constitutionality of the Espionage Act. Their appeal was denied and the Rosenbergs were executed on June 19, 1953, at Sing Sing Prison, NY.

Time: 3 to 4 class periods

Objectives:

- To analyze the causes and effects of the postwar Communist scare.

- To analyze the techniques of McCarthyism.

- To interpret information obtained from a graph.

Materials Needed:

Documents 22-25
Sound recordings D and F
Worksheet 6

Procedures:

1. Play sound recordings D and F and duplicate and distribute documents 22-24. Allow students time to listen to and to read carefully the materials, using the Sound Recording, Cartoon, and Written Document Analysis worksheets if appropriate.

   The McCarthy era has been compared by many to the hysteria of the Salem witch trials. In her book *The Devil in Massachusetts: A Modern Inquiry into Salem Witch Trials*, Marion Starkey develops the hypothesis that such periods of persecution follow a pattern. A genuine problem generates such fear that authorities curtail liberties of people who are poor, lacking in status, or unpopular. The persecution spreads to people who consider themselves middle-class, "respectable" folk, then rages on to consume the powerful and wealthy before it wanes. Ask students to identify whether and how each document fits into this general pattern and to comment on the following passage written in Germany in 1945 by Pastor Martin Niemoller:

   > In Germany the Nazis came for the Communists and I did not speak up because I was not a Communist. Then they came for the Jews, and I did not speak up because I was not a Jew. Then they came for the trade unionists, and I did not speak up because I was not a trade unionist. Then they came for the Catholics and I did not speak up because I was a Protestant. Then they came for ME. And by that time there was no one left to speak up for me.

2. The term "McCarthyism" has come to mean a reckless and unsupported attack against people by the use of such techniques as guilt by association, widespread and dubious imposition of loyalty oaths, scrutiny by secret informants, blacklists, suppression of citizens' freedoms of speech and assembly, interrogation and intimidation of the accused by public committees, and submission of unsupported allegations against the accused. Ask students to read document 22, underlining examples of these techniques. When the students have completed marking up their letters, ask them to share their findings as a class. Ask students to comment on how the other sound recordings and documents illustrate the methods of McCarthyism. Ask the following question: If McCarthy's allegations of Communist infiltration in government had been correct, would his means have been justified?

3. Duplicate and distribute worksheet 6 and post document 25 on a bulletin board. Ask students to examine the chart in small groups and then to complete the worksheet.

4. Ask for two students to volunteer to study the Rosenbergs' case and to argue the case, one as government prosecutor and the other as defense attorney for the Rosenbergs. Allow each side 10 minutes to present their case, 2 minutes for cross-examination, and 5 minutes for rebuttal and final argument. Poll the onlooking students by directing them to go to the prosecutor's side of the room if convinced by the prosecutor, or to the defense's side of the room if convinced by the defense attorney. Ask each student to write one paragraph expressing his or her opinion, supported by facts, on what the verdict should be. Collect paragraphs as the students leave class. At the beginning of the next class, announce the results of the written verdicts, noting if there are differences between the public and secret polls of the verdict. Give the actual verdict and explain that it was appealed. Ask students to identify what constitutional issues in the case would have made it eligible for the Supreme Court's October 1952 term.

5. In a general class discussion, pose to students the following questions:

   a. Can true democracy exist only when extremes of opinion are tolerated?

   b. Is outlawing any political faction consistent with the First Amendment?

   c. Is "making America pure as we can make it" an ideal consistent with freedom and democracy?

   d. What is pluralism? What is its role in a democracy?

   Worksheet 6 answers: 1 a. 320 b. 40 c. 1,480 d. 1,000 e. 0 f. 50 g. 10 h. 210 i. 500 j. 0 k. 10 l. 90 m. 0; 2 a. 2,330 b. 870; 3. answers will vary; 4. answers will vary

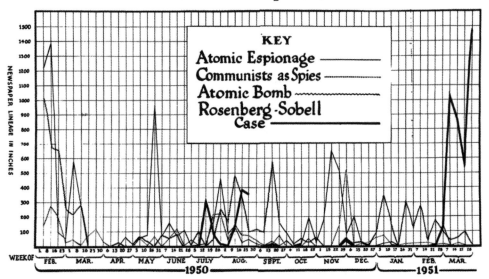

QUANTITATIVE REPORTAGE
Feb. 1, 1950 to April, 3, 1951

KEY
Atomic Espionage ————
Communists as Spies ·····
Atomic Bomb ～～～～
Rosenberg-Sobell Case ————

Exercise 7: Soviet Espionage and an Atmosphere of Distrust

Worksheet 6

Directions: Study document 25 and answer the following questions.

1. How much newspaper lineage dealt with the topic of:

   the Rosenbergs on July 12, 1950 _____

   the Rosenbergs on Nov. 29, 1950 _____

   the Rosenbergs on Mar. 28, 1951 _____

   the atomic bomb on Feb. 1, 1950 _____

   the atomic bomb on July 12, 1950 _____

   the atomic bomb on Nov. 29, 1950 _____

   the atomic bomb on Mar. 28, 1951 _____

   the Communists on July 19, 1950 _____

   the Communists on Nov. 29, 1950 _____

   the Communists on Mar. 28, 1951 _____

   Atomic espionage on July 12, 1950 _____

   Atomic espionage on Nov. 29, 1950 _____

   Atomic espionage on Mar. 28, 1951 _____

2. Total number of lines printed on all four issues on:

   Feb. 8, 1950 was _____

   Aug. 9, 1950 was _____

3. Examine July 5-August 23, 1950, the time period when Julius Rosenberg and then Ethel were arrested on suspicion of espionage. Was there active coverage of all four issues at the time?

   _____

   _____

   How might active coverage or lack of it have affected the March 1951 trial?

   _____

   _____

4. How might the Rosenbergs' lawyers have used the chart as evidence that their case had been influenced by pretrial publicity?

   _____

   _____

Exercise 8
The Korean War

Note to the Teacher:

In Korea the cold war turned red hot on June 25, 1950, when the North Korean People's Army (NKPA) of 90,000 troops, supported by 150 Russian made T-34 tanks, crossed the 38th parallel and invaded the non-Communist, southern part of Korea. Their goal was to overthrow the Republic of Korea, the U.S.-backed government of Dr. Syngman Rhee. In response President Truman asked the United Nations for a resolution calling for a cease-fire and asking member nations to "furnish such assistance to the Republic of Korea (South Korea) as may be necessary." **Document 26** is a memorandum outlining the military situation in Korea on June 27, 1950, and ordering the removal of restrictions on the use of U.S. naval and air forces in the Far East. This action committed the United States to the military defense of the Republic of Korea. To honor this commitment, Truman chose to declare the existence of a national emergency rather than a state of war. His hope was to limit the conflict to the Korean peninsula. **Document 27** is President Truman's proclamation to the American people explaining the need for increased effort to defeat this "grave threat to the peace of the world."

On July 8, 1950, U.S. Gen. Douglas MacArthur, serving in Japan as Supreme Commander of Allied Powers (SCAP), was named to command the combined U.N. armed forces in Korea. This combined force included the soldiers in the army of the Republic of Korea as well as troops from the United States and other U.N. participants. This patchwork army retreated down the Korean peninsula into a defensive perimeter, roughly 50 miles wide, around the southern port city of Pusan. On September 15, 1950, MacArthur launched a counterattack with an amphibious landing behind the North Korean lines at Inchon on the western coast. MacArthur's daring end run caught the NKPA by surprise, with their front lines weakened and their supply lines overextended.

By September 26 the U.N. forces had recaptured the Republic of Korea's capital city of Seoul, had pushed the North Koreans back across the 38th parallel, and were advancing toward the Chinese border along the Yalu River. One of the operations in the advance north was an airborne assault on Munsan-ni in North Korea on October 20, 1950, by the 187th Regimental Combat Team. Accompanying this team was Lt. Col. Wes MacPheron, whose voice is heard on **sound recording G**. MacPheron recorded the prejump officers' briefing, the intelligence briefing the night before the mission, the parachute jump, actual combat between troops and the North Koreans, and a press conference by the U.S. commander at the conclusion of the assault.

With MacArthur advancing toward the Yalu River, China's Foreign Minister Chou En-lai warned that the Chinese would intervene to help their neighbors. Alarmed, Truman met with MacArthur at Wake Island and was assured by MacArthur that the Chinese would not intervene. On November 26, 1950, however, units of the Chinese Communist army attacked across the Yalu, forcing the U.N. forces into retreat. For months the battle lines moved back and forth in stalemate along the Korean peninsula.

Truman, realizing that the American people would not support a protracted war, began secret negotiations with the North Koreans aimed at finding "an acceptable solution" to the Korean situation. **Document 28** is a memorandum outlining the U.S. position regarding an armistice. On March 20, 1951, MacArthur, tiring of the U.S. policy of limited warfare in Korea, proposed to attack the Chinese mainland. This threat undermined the armistice negotiations and led to further fighting. It was the March 25 statement (see exercise 4, document 15) that forced Truman to replace MacArthur as U.N. commander with Gen. Matthew Ridgway.

The Korean stalemate continued into the Eisenhower administration, with an armistice finally achieved on July 27, 1953. This agreement maintained the status quo, with most of the provisions identical to those that could have been obtained in 1951.

Time: 1 to 3 class periods

Objectives:

- To determine the chronology of events of the Korean war.

- To explain how and why the United States entered the Korean war.

- To compare, contrast, and evaluate the historical accuracy of a fictionalized account of a historical event.

Materials Needed:

Documents 26-28
Sound recording G
Worksheet 7

Procedures:

1. Duplicate and distribute documents 26-28 and worksheet 7. Ask students to review the documents along with the section on the Korean war in their textbooks. Direct them to complete the time line of significant events in the Korean war on worksheet 7.

2. Play sound recording G for the class. If appropriate, ask students to complete the Sound Recording Analysis worksheet. As a class consider the following questions:
   a. What was the status of U.N. forces in Korea in October of 1950? (Refer to a map in your textbook)
   b. Who were the Americans fighting against in October 1950?
   c. Whom did most Americans identify as the enemy in Korea?
   d. What effect do you think having a war correspondent on the operation described on the sound recording might have had?
   e. Does the operation seem to be a U.N. or a U.S. one? Support your answer with examples.
   f. What was the most interesting or attention-holding incident in this recording?

3. Ask students to review the status of U.S. and U.N. forces and conditions in the two Koreas today and then to draft a proposal for a peace treaty to bring to a conclusion the hostilities that have continued since the armistice of 1953.

4. Ask students to evaluate the impact of a Presidential proclamation of emergency in lieu of a congressional declaration of war on the constitutional separation of powers and checks and balances.

5. Extended activity: Encourage students to watch reruns of the television series M*A*S*H, to compare and contrast its representation of the war with the historical record that they have studied, and to judge the historical accuracy of the television series. Students may wish to focus on one episode and one issue, such as the black and white interview of M*A*S*H characters by a U.S. television reporter, which they might contrast with historic media coverage of the war illustrated by sound recording G.

8

Exercise 8: The Korean War

Worksheet 7

Directions: Use information in documents 26-28 and your textbook to complete the time line.

1950	_____
June 25	_____ NKPA troops cross the 38th parallel
June 27	_____ Document 26, military situation in Korea
July	_____
August	_____
September	_____
October 20	_____ Sound recording G, assault on Munsan-ni
November	_____
December	_____
1951	_____
January	_____
February	_____
March 25	_____ MacArthur threatens to attack Chinese mainland
April	_____
May	_____
June	_____
August	_____
October	_____
December	_____
1952	_____
1953	_____
July 27	_____ Korean armistice signed

Exercise 9
Harry S. Truman

Note to the Teacher:

Two memorable events personally marked Truman's years in the White House – the 1948 election for President and the assassination attempt on his life in 1950. For the 1948 Presidential campaign, the Republican Party had coalesced behind New York Governor Thomas E. Dewey, who was nominated at the party's convention. On the other hand, Harry S. Truman headed a badly fragmented Democratic Party. Although the President was selected as the Democratic standard-bearer at the convention, his fortunes were damaged when southern Democrats walked out in protest of the civil rights plank of the party platform. These so-called Dixiecrats organized the States' Rights Democratic Party and selected South Carolina Governor J. Strom Thurmond as their Presidential candidate. Additional defections occurred when Henry A. Wallace, former Vice President under Franklin D. Roosevelt, led some liberal Democrats into a new Progressive Party. By September, pollsters, columnists, cartoonists, radio commentators, and political experts predicted a landslide victory by Dewey. Undaunted, Truman traveled nearly 32,000 miles cross country in a whistlestop railroad campaign tour **(document 29)**, assailing what he asserted was the "do-nothing" Republican 80th Congress' failure to help the average citizen. On November 2, 1948, Truman defeated Dewey in one of the most dramatic upsets in the political history of the United States. **Document 30**, the cartoon titled "—and on Two Legs," concedes the embarrassment of the "experts" on Truman's unexpected victory.

Two years later, on November 1, 1950, Puerto Rican Nationalists attempted to assassinate President Truman in front of Blair House, the temporary residence of the Trumans while the White House was being renovated. Leslie Coffelt, a White House police officer, died in the attempt, as well as Grieselio Torresola, one of the assailants. Oscar Collazo, the other attacker, was convicted of Coffelt's murder and was sentenced to death, although Truman commuted the sentence to life imprisonment in 1952. The attempt on Truman's life was loosely coordinated with a nearly simultaneous attack on Puerto Rico's Governor Luis Munõz Marin, which was also unsuccessful. Expressions of regret and concern flooded the White House following the incident, including many messages from Puerto Rico, such as the one from the president of the Asociacion de Industriales Angel Suárez **(document 31)**.

Time: 1 class period

Objectives:

- To examine the election of 1948.

- To trace changes in the status of Puerto Rico from territory to commonwealth.

Materials Needed:

Documents 29-31
Worksheet 8

9

Procedures:

1. Provide each student with copies of documents 29-31 and worksheet 8. After the students complete the worksheet, ask them the following questions:

   a. Why do you think Truman won the election?

   b. Why was Truman at Blair House rather than the White House when the assassination attempt occurred?

   c. What other Presidents of the United States have survived assassination attempts?

   d. Truman was fond of taking a daily walk to meet the public. How can security needs be balanced with the need for the President to have contact with the public?

2. Extended activity: Ask students to research the changes in the status of Puerto Rico from the end of the Spanish-American War to the present. They should consider the following questions:

   a. What economic changes have occurred since the initiation of Operation Bootstrap in 1947?

   b. What political changes occurred when Puerto Rico became a commonwealth in 1953?

   c. What obligations and rights did Puerto Rico have as a territory of the United States? What obligations and rights does Puerto Rico have as a commonwealth associated with the United States?

   d. Some political activists want Puerto Rico to apply for statehood, others want it to continue as a commonwealth, and others want it to become an independent nation. What are the advantages and disadvantages of each alternative for Puerto Rico and for the United States? In your judgement, which alternative should govern the policy of the United States?

Exercise 9: Harry S. Truman

Worksheet 8

Directions: Study documents 29-31 carefully. Check either "True" or "False" in the column to the left of each statement.

True   **False**

_____   _____   1. Angel Suárez regretted the attempt on Truman's life.

_____   _____   2. The assassination attempt occurred at Truman's house in Independence, MO.

_____   _____   3. Puerto Ricans were exempt from military service in the Korean war.

_____   _____   4. Suárez represented an association of Puerto Rican industrialists.

_____   _____   5. There was little support for U.S. institutions in Puerto Rico.

_____   _____   6. The Wallace vote and Thurmond vote helped Truman to win the election.

_____   _____   7. Poll takers were embarrassed by Truman's victory.

_____   _____   8. Gamblers won a great deal of money betting against Truman.

_____   _____   9. The whistlestop campaign was conducted on television.

_____   _____   10. Whistlestop campaigning brought Truman into direct contact with the public.

Exercise 10
Civil Rights

Note to the Teacher:

World War II brought more substantial changes to the position of minorities in U.S. society than World War I had brought. Some employers who before World War II showed no interest in hiring minorities sought them out during the war in the face of wartime labor shortages. These employers were willing to look beyond prejudices in order to help defend the nation. In addition to filling jobs on the home front, blacks, Native Americans, and other minorities answered the call to arms and marched off to defend a democracy in which most minorities could not fully participate.

Realizing the need for total mobilization of the U.S. population, President Franklin D. Roosevelt established by executive order on June 25, 1941, the Fair Employment Practice Committee (FEPC). The mission of the committee was "to encourage full participation in the nation's defense program by all citizens . . . regardless of race, creed, color, or national origin." Throughout the war the FEPC monitored the labor market and acted to curb discriminatory practices by employers and unions. Despite bipartisan support, bills to create a permanent FEPC when the war ended were blocked by southern and conservative legislators. The committee ceased operations on June 30, 1946.

President Truman felt that the work of the Fair Employment Practice Committee was far from completed. **Document 32**, a letter from G. Raymond Booth, Executive Director of the Council for Civic Unity, outlining the conditions of minority employment in Los Angeles County, supported the President's belief. To improve the conditions of minorities in the United States, Truman formed the Committee on Civil Rights to study the problem and make recommendations. In October 1947, the President's committee issued its report. The committee called for stronger civil rights legislation, the creation of a civil rights division within the Justice Department, federal laws against lynching, and home rule for the District of Columbia. In 1948 Truman asked Congress to enact legislation to correct the deficiencies enumerated by the Committee on Civil Rights. He also issued two executive orders, one that called for fair employment practices throughout the federal government and the other for desegregation of the armed forces. **Document 33** is Executive Order 9981, which provided for "equal treatment and opportunity for all persons in the armed services." The order desegregating the military was to be carried out "as rapidly as possible."

On the heels of the executive orders integrating the civilian and military bureaucracies, Truman inserted a strong civil rights plank into the 1948 Democratic Party platform. Though written in general terms, this plank specifically endorsed the legislation recommended by Truman and the Committee on Civil Rights.

Following his re-election, Truman unsuccessfully tried to persuade Congress to accept his civil rights package. Firmly believing that the Constitution guaranteed individual liberty and equal protection under the law for all citizens, the President committed the federal government to the task of ensuring constitutional civil rights.

President Truman realized that segregation fostered discrimination. Not only were minorities denied individual civil and political liberties in a segregated society, they were also denied personal dignity. **Document 35** is a newspaper article describing the funeral of Sgt. John R. Rice, a World War II veteran who died defending a bridgehead near Pusan, Korea. When his family tried to bury him in a Sioux City, IA, cemetery, they were denied permission because Rice was a Native American. After Truman intervened, Sergeant Rice was buried in Arlington National Cemetery with full military honors.

Postwar U.S. society was in a time of transition. Blacks and other minorities were crossing the color barrier and taking jobs in areas that had only recently been all white. **Document 34** is a photograph of one such person, Jackie Robinson. Robinson, a former standout running back on the integrated UCLA football team, signed a contract on October 28, 1945, to play baseball with Branch Rickey's Brooklyn Dodgers two years later. He became the first black man to play in major league baseball.

Integration did not go smoothly. Robinson faced hatred, prejudice, and abuse from players and fans alike. He channeled his frustration into superb play on the field, being named rookie of the year in 1947 and National League Most Valuable Player in 1949. By 1950, baseball had opened its doors to 49 black ballplayers, including Don Newcombe, Roy Campanella, Monte Irvin, Larry Doby, and Satchel Paige.

There were still many battles to be fought and won before minorities would enjoy equal rights under the law, but the seeds of change were sown in the Truman years. President Truman's contribution to the civil rights movement was to make the federal government the agent to ensure equal rights for all citizens of the United States, regardless of race, creed, or national origin.

Time: 2 to 3 class periods

Objectives:

- To assess the impact of the government's desegregation program on other sectors of American life.

- To consider the effects of segregation and desegregation on Americans.

- To identify point of view.

Materials Needed:

Documents 32-35
Worksheet 9

Procedures:

1. Duplicate documents 32 and 35 and worksheet 9 and then distribute a copy of each to the students. After pupils have completed the assignment, answer any questions they may have. (Note that the worksheet uses the language of the document; i.e., Negroes for black Americans.)

2. Make an overlay for the overhead projector of document 33 and show it to the class. Ask students to speculate on the impact of the desegregation order on a military base and on a segregated town adjacent to a military base. Ask students to play the roles of a black recruit, a white recruit, an NCO in charge of inducting recruits, a base commander, a USO club manager, a provost marshal (responsible for declaring Jim Crow establishments off-limits to military personnel), an owner of a cafe in town, and a pastor of a church following Truman's desegregation order in 1948. Ask another student to conduct an interview with each person. Suggested questions for the interview might include:

   a. How has desegregation of the armed forces affected you?

   b. What changes have you had to make because of desegregation (e.g., housing)?

   c. How has desegregation affected the efficiency of the military units?

   d. How has desegregation affected your business?

e. Has desegregation changed the relationship between the military base and the town?

3. Show document 34 to your students and describe Jackie Robinson's achievements. Traditionally, athletics has been thought to provide a route for economic mobility for minorities. Ask students to research the impact of both segregation and desegregation on various sports as well as on individual athletes. Suggested areas of inquiry might include:

a. baseball

b. basketball

c. boxing

d. football

e. tennis

f. track

Ask students to share their findings through oral or written reports.

EXECUTIVE ORDER

ESTABLISHING THE PRESIDENT'S COMMITTEE ON
EQUALITY OF TREATMENT AND OPPORTUNITY IN
THE ARMED SERVICES

WHEREAS it is essential that there be maintained in the armed services of the United States the highest standards of democracy, with equality of treatment and opportunity for all those who serve in our country's defense:

NOW, THEREFORE, by virtue of the authority vested in me as President of the United States, by the Constitution and the statutes of the United States, and as Commander in Chief of the armed services, it is hereby ordered as follows:

1. It is hereby declared to be the policy of the President that there shall be equality of treatment and opportunity for all persons in the armed services without regard to race, color, religion or national origin. This policy shall be put into effect as rapidly as possible, having due regard to the time required to effectuate any necessary changes without impairing efficiency or morale.

2. There shall be created in the National Military Establishment an advisory committee to be known as the President's Committee on Equality of Treatment and Opportunity in the Armed Services, which shall be composed of seven members to be designated by the President.

3. The Committee is authorized on behalf of the President to examine into the rules, procedures and practices of the armed services in order to determine in what respect such rules, procedures and practices may be altered or improved with a view to carrying out the policy of this order. The Committee shall confer and advise with the Secretary of Defense, the Secretary

Exercise 10: Civil Rights

Worksheet 9

Directions: Use information from documents 32 and 35 to complete the worksheet.

Document 32

1. Why did employment conditions for minorities improve during World War II?
   _____

2. Which minority groups benefited economically during World War II?
   _____

3. Which minority group was hurt worst, economically, during World War II?
   _____

4. What minority group was most successful after the war? How does Booth account for this success?
   _____

5. What sources of racial tension were foreseen in the Booth letter from Los Angeles?
   _____

6. What stereotypes are included in this letter?
   _____

7. What is the point of view of G. Raymond Booth in this letter?
   _____

8. Make a bar graph showing the number of Negroes, Mexican-Americans, Jews, and Japanese-Americans in Los Angeles County in 1946.
   _____

Document 35

1. What happened at Sergeant Rice's first funeral service?
   _____

2. Why was he denied burial at the Sioux City, IA, Memorial Park Cemetery?
   _____

3. Were segregated cemeteries common in 1951?
   _____

4. What is the point of view of this article from the *Cincinnati Enquirer*?
   _____
   _____

Exercise 11
Life in Postwar America: A Photographic Study

Note to the Teacher:

Following World War II, the United States underwent economic expansion, technological development, and population growth that transformed the American way of life. Increased productivity by veterans returning to civilian jobs triggered a new prosperity and reduced the average workweek to 40 hours. This affluence and leisure fueled consumer demand for housing, products, and entertainment. In 1946 only 7,000 television sets were sold, but by 1950 sales approached seven million. Standard designs and features in new houses lowered builders' costs and enabled them to sell houses at affordable prices to couples, many of whom had wartime savings or "G.I. Bill" benefits. The Lustron home, advertised in **document 39**, was a prefabricated home, constructed with porcelain enameled steel panels, that sold for about $4,000. Postwar resumption of automobile and tire production and highway improvements spurred rapid growth of housing projects in suburban areas. Renewed mobility also led to a proliferation of service stations, motels, and fast-food restaurants. **Documents 36-40** capture many of the changes in postwar America.

Time: 1 to 2 class periods

Objectives:

- To analyze a photograph for information.

- To describe changes in American life following World War II.

Materials Needed:

Documents 36-40
Photograph Analysis worksheet, p. 14
Worksheet 10

Procedures:

1. Divide the class into groups of five students each. Duplicate the set of five documents for each group and a Photograph Analysis worksheet for each student. Direct each student to analyze one photograph in the set. Duplicate Worksheet 10 and distribute a copy of it to each student; direct students to circulate the documents within the group as they each complete the worksheet. Once the worksheets are complete, review each document with the class.

2. Extended activity: Ask students to collect information on American life in the postwar years from documents 36-40, their textbooks, adults who recall the time period, and other primary and secondary sources. Assign a letter-writing exercise giving the following directions: Imagine you are a middle-class American teenager living in suburbia in 1952. Write a letter to an overseas pen pal describing your way of life.

Exercise 11: Life in Postwar America: A Photographic Study

Worksheet 10

Directions: Use information from documents 36-40 to complete the worksheet.

Document 36

1. What postwar housing needs were satisfied by developments such as this one?

   _____

2. What features does each house seem to share?

   _____

3. What effect does this development have on the countryside?

   _____

4. What features do these houses lack that you would expect to see in a housing development today?

   _____

Document 37

1. An influential book on interior design of the postwar period was *Easier Living* by Russell Wright. How does this interior design reflect the ideal of easier living?

   _____

2. What values are conveyed in this furniture style, arrangement, and interior?

   _____

3. What features of this interior seem old-fashioned?

   _____

4. What features are present that you wouldn't expect today?

   _____

5. What features are missing that you would expect to find today?

   _____

Document 38

1. What features of the television set does this advertisement promote?

   _____

2. Why is Hopalong Cassidy used in the advertisement?

   _____

3. Why is the young boy in a cowboy outfit used in this advertisement?

   _____

4. Who is the target audience for this advertisement?

   _____

5. What features of the television set seem old-fashioned to you?

   _____

Document 39

1. What need does this advertisement say the product fulfills?

   _____

2. What forms of advertising did Lustron use?

   _____

3. How many rooms are in this house? How many people do you think it will comfortably accommodate?

   _____

4. Who is the target audience for this advertisement?

   _____

5. What items in this advertisement seem old-fashioned?

   _____

6. What can you ascertain about the popular notion of family life from this advertisement?

   _____

Document 40

1. What was Studebaker?

   _____

2. What features of this service station seem old-fashioned?

   _____

3. Ask a person who recalls the postwar years what premiums were and why they were free.

   _____

4. Ask a person who recalls the postwar years what the price of gasoline was.

   _____

5. Ask a person who recalls the postwar years what sort of premiums were offered at gas stations.

   _____

6. What do these responses tell you about the role of the automobile then and now?

   _____

   _____

Time Line

1945	February 4-11	FDR, Churchill, and Stalin hold Yalta Conference and formulate postwar plans
	March 14	Iwo Jima is captured by U.S. forces
	April 1	Okinawa is invaded by U.S. forces
	April 12	FDR dies of stroke at Warm Springs, GA
	April 12	Harry S. Truman is sworn in as 33rd U.S. President
	May 8	V-E Day
	June 21	U.S. Marines secure Okinawa
	July 16	United States explodes first atomic bomb at Alamogordo, NM
	July 17	Potsdam Conference is held to plan occupation of Germany
	July 28	U.S. Senate ratifies U.N. charter
	August 6	United States drops atomic bomb on Hiroshima
	August 9	United States drops atomic bomb on Nagasaki
	August 14	V-J Day
	August 20	War Production Board is largely dismantled, returning economy to peacetime basis
	October 24	U.N. charter comes into force
	November 20	International Military Tribunal begins trials of major German war criminals, including Hermann Goering, Joachim von Ribbentrop, and Field Marshall Wilhelm Keitel. U S. prosecutor is Associate Justice Robert Jackson
1946		ENIAC, the first truly automatic computer, is developed, based on work done at the University of Pennsylvania
	January 10	First U.N. General Assembly meets
	January 10	Radar signals are sent to the moon and reflected back
	January 19	International Military Tribunal is established to try Japanese war leaders
	February 22	George F. Kennan sends famous telegram to the Secretary of State outlining the "character, tactics, motivation and ambitions" of the Soviet Union
	March 5	Winston Churchill delivers "iron curtain" speech at Fulton, MO
	April	Full-scale civil war begins in China
	May 21	Truman takes over coal mines following strike by United Mine Workers
	November 9	Truman ends all wage and price controls except for those on rents, sugar, and rice
	December 5	Executive Order 9802 creates the President's Committee on Civil Rights
1947		Polaroid Land camera is invented by Edwin Herbert Land
		Jet-propelled fighters and bombers are developed by the U.S. Air Force
		Tennessee Williams' play *A Streetcar Named Desire* is staged for the first time

March 12	The Truman Doctrine is made public in a Presidential request to Congress for aid to Greece and Turkey	
April 11	Jackie Robinson is signed by the Brooklyn Dodgers	
June 5	Secretary of State George C. Marshall, seeking to revive world economy, proposes what comes to be known as the Marshall Plan in an address at Harvard University	
June 20	Truman vetoes the Taft-Hartley Act, seen as anti-labor	
June 23	Taft-Hartley Act passed by Congress over Truman's veto	
July	"The Source of Soviet Conduct" by "X" [George F. Kennan] appears in *Foreign Affairs*	
July 18	Presidential Succession Act is passed, amending an 1886 law. The order of succession to the Presidency after the Vice President is the Speaker of the House first and President pro tempore of the Senate second	
1948	Babe (George Herman) Ruth, b. 1895, dies	
	Tubeless tires are introduced by Goodrich	
	Transistor is invented at Bell Laboratories	
	33 1/3 rpm microgroove record is invented by Peter C. Goldmark	
	Alfred C. Kinsey publishes *Sexual Behavior in the Human Male*	
	Norman Mailer publishes *The Naked and the Dead*	
	The Organization of American States (OAS) is chartered	
April 1	Stalin orders blockade of West Berlin	
May 14	New State of Israel is proclaimed by the United Nations	
June 24	Berlin airlift begins attempt to break Soviet blockade without force	
July 30	Executive Order 9981 is issued, aimed at ending segregation in the armed services	
November 2	Truman is elected President despite polls and newspaper headlines proclaiming Thomas Dewey the winner	
1949	V-8 engine is introduced	
	Arthur Miller's play *Death of a Salesman* is staged for the first time The movie *Intruder in the Dust* is released	
January 20	Truman announces Point Four program, providing economic aid to underdeveloped nations, in his inaugural address	
April 4	NATO, the North Atlantic Treaty Organization, is formed by a military alliance	
September 23	Truman reveals that Russia has detonated atomic bomb	
October 1– December 7	Mao Tse-tung and Chou En-lai establish the People's Republic of China, driving Chiang Kai-shek's nationalist government to Taiwan	
1950	Census shows U.S. population at 150,697,000	
	Ralph Bunche receives Nobel Peace Prize for work as U.N. mediator in the Middle East crisis	
	Jackson Pollock breaks new ground with his expressionist painting "Mural on Indian Red Ground"	

January	Truman orders work to proceed on hydrogen bomb	
January 21	Alger Hiss is sentenced to 5-year prison term for perjury	
February 9	Senator Joseph McCarthy announces that he has names of 205 communists who work in the U.S. State Department	
June 25	North Korean forces invade South Korea	
June 27	Truman sends 35 military advisors to Vietnam	
September 15	U.N. forces under Gen. Douglas MacArthur capture Inchon, Korea	
September 23	Internal Security Act of 1950 (McCarran Act), which requires registration of Communists, passes over Truman's veto	
November 1	Two Puerto Rican nationalists attempt to assassinate Truman at Blair House, Washington, DC	
October 26	Chinese communists enter Korean war	
1951	Bobby Thomson, New York Giants, hits 9th-inning home run, defeating the Brooklyn Dodgers for the World Series pennant	
	J.D. Salinger publishes *The Catcher in the Rye*	
	Herman Wouk publishes *The Caine Mutiny*	
February 26	22nd amendment is passed, limiting a President to two terms in office	
April	Truman dismisses Gen. Douglas MacArthur for disobeying his orders	
April 5	Julius and Ethel Rosenberg are sentenced to death for stealing atomic secrets	
September 4	First simultaneous nationwide TV broadcast	
September 8	Japanese Peace Treaty is signed at a meeting held in San Francisco	
1952	Ernest Hemingway publishes *The Old Man and the Sea*	
	Ralph Ellison publishes *Invisible Man*	
April 8	Truman orders government seizure of steel mills in order to prevent a strike	
September 23	Vice Presidential candidate Richard M. Nixon gives "Checkers" speech on TV	
November 1	United States explodes first hydrogen bomb	
1953	CinemaScope is introduced by 20th Century Fox in *The Robe*	
	3-D is introduced in movie films	
	Arthur Miller's play *The Crucible* is staged for the first time	
January 20	Dwight D. Eisenhower is inaugurated as 34th U.S. President	
July 27	Korean armistice is signed	
August 20	Soviet Union announces it has tested a hydrogen bomb	
December 8	Link between cancer and cigarette smoking is reported by Dr. Alton Ochsner	

Annotated Bibliography

Bailey, Thomas A. *The Marshall Plan Summer: An Eyewitness Report on Europe and the Russians in 1947.* Stanford, CA: Hoover Institution Press, 1977.

Commissioned to tour Europe by the U.S. National War College in the summer of 1947, Bailey has compiled "a diary. . .a primary source" based on his eyewitness accounts of conditions in Europe on the eve of the Marshall Plan.

_____. *The Pugnacious Presidents: White House Warriors on Parade.* New York: Free Press, 1980.

This volume looks at the way U.S. Presidents from George Washington to Jimmy Carter have dealt with war and the threat of war. Specifically, it discusses how Truman's handling of the cold war and the Korean war compares to actions of other U.S. Presidents in similar situations.

Bentley, Eric. *Rallying Cries: Three Plays.* Evanston, IL: Northwestern University Press, 1987.

One of the plays, *Are You Now Or Have You Ever Been,* recreates the 1947 Un-American Activities Committee's investigation of the "Hollywood Ten" for possible affiliation with the Communist Party.

Bernstein, Barton J., ed. *Politics and Policies of the Truman Administration.* Chicago: Quadrangle Books, 1970.

This volume consists of essays that take a critical view of the Truman administration's foreign policy, decisions on internal security, and civil rights programs. These essays assume that the reader has a general knowledge of the history of the Truman era.

_____. *The Atomic Bomb: The Critical Issues.* Boston: Little Brown, 1976.

Was the A-bomb needed to end the war in the Pacific? Did "atomic diplomacy" play a role? What is the moral significance of Hiroshima and Nagasaki? These and other questions relating to the decision to drop the A-bomb are addressed in this volume of essays.

_____. and Matusow, Allen J., eds. *The Truman Administration: A Documentary History.* New York: Harper & Row, 1966.

This volume uses memorandums, reports, the *Congressional Record,* and other primary sources to assemble first-hand reactions to crucial decisions in the Truman era regarding the A-bomb, wage and price controls, the Fair Deal, the Cold War, China, internal security, and the Korean war.

Burns, Richard D. *Harry S. Truman: A Bibliography of His Times and Presidency.* Wilmington, DE: Scholarly Resources, Inc., 1984.

This is an excellent, selective bibliography. It is topically comprehensive and contains a chronology, an author index, a subject index, and illustrations, making it an easy reference tool.

Collins, David R. *Harry S. Truman: People's President.* Champaign, IL: Garrard, 1975.

This is a volume of brief, well-written essays interpreting Truman's Presidency.

Etzold, Thomas H. and Gaddis, John Lewis, eds. *Containment: Documents on American Policy and Strategy, 1945-1950.* New York: Columbia University Press, 1978.

Using recently declassified documents, including NSC-68, the editors seek to illustrate the political and military considerations that went into the policy and strategy of containment from 1945 to 1950. This study gives students a chance to compare recently declassified documents with contemporary unclassified information for the period.

Faber, Doris. *Harry Truman*. New York: Abelard-Schuman, 1972.

>This biography recounts Truman's childhood, his time in the army, the years he spent in the Senate, and his Presidency.

Ferrell, Robert H. *Harry S. Truman and the Modern American Presidency*. Boston: Little, Brown, 1983.

>This account of Truman takes a favorable view of his experiences in local and national politics and his role in the early years of the cold war.

_____, ed. *Off-the-Record: The Private Papers of Harry S. Truman*. Columbia: University of Missouri Press, 1997.

>Included in this volume are letters, entries from Truman's diary, and memorandums covering the period from 1947 to 1971.

_____., ed. *The Autobiography of Harry S. Truman*. Boulder, CO: Colorado Associated University Press, 1980.

>This "autobiography" is fashioned from Truman's handwritten accounts of his life. Readers can compare Truman's view of himself with those views found in secondary sources.

Freedom to Serve: Equality of Treatment and Opportunity in the Armed Services. U.S. President's Committee Report. Washington, DC: U.S. Government Printing Office, 1950.

>This committee reviewed the implementation of Executive Order 9981 (July 26, 1948), by which Truman ordered that all persons in the armed services be given equal treatment and opportunity without regard to race, color, religion, or national origin.

Fried, Richard M. *Nightmare in Red: The McCarthy Era in Perspective*. New York: Oxford University Press, 1990.

>A comprehensive narrative account of the red scare of the 1950s, this work traces anticommunism in America from the New Deal through World War II and the 1950s and into the 1960s. The book discusses not only the major political events associated with McCarthyism but also looks at the effect of McCarthyism on the lives of ordinary Americans.

Goldstein, Alvin H. *Unquiet Death of Julius and Ethel Rosenberg*. New York: Lawrence Hill, 1975.

>Goldstein interviewed 200 persons for a public television documentary. This volume contains his impressions based on those interviews.

Griffith, Robert. *The Politics of Fear: Joseph R. McCarthy and the Senate*. 2d ed. Amherst: University of Massachusettes Press, 1987.

>Griffith discusses the social conditions, party politics, and historical U.S. attitudes toward radicalism that led to the preeminence of McCarthy.

Hamby, Alonzo L. *Man of the People: A Life of Harry S Truman*. New York: Oxford University Press, 1995.

>A delicate portrait of the complex Harry Truman, this book is thoroughly researched and documented. It carefully illustrates the many sides to Truman's character from his childhood to his death. Its length and academic writing style may prove discouraging for students.

Harry S. Truman Library. *Historical Materials in the Harry S. Truman Library*. Independence, MO: Harry S. Truman Library, 1987.

>Lists and brief descriptions of primary source materials available in the Truman Presidential Library holdings. These include manuscripts, microfilm, and oral history interviews. Inquiries about conditions of use and available copies of these materials should be addressed to: Harry S. Truman Library, Independence, MO 64050.

Hartmann, Susan M. *Truman and the 80th Congress*. Columbia: University of Missouri Press, 1971.

> The 80th Congress' failure to pass much of Truman's Fair Deal legislation led him to label it a "do-nothing Congress" in the Presidential election campaign of 1948. Hartmann examines some of the foreign-related and domestic legislation sent to the 80th Congress by Truman.

Hedley, John H. *Harry S. Truman: The "Little" Man from Missouri*. Woodbury, NY: Barron's, 1979.

> A political biography that focuses on Truman's role in international affairs. This account contains a historiographical essay (chapter 8, "The Verdict of History") that is particularly useful.

Heller, Francis H., ed. *The Truman White House: The Administration of the Presidency, 1945-1953*. Lawrence: Regents Press of Kansas, 1980.

> This volume is based on papers presented at a conference sponsored by the Harry S. Truman Library Institute and attended by 22 persons who had served in Truman's administration.

Hiroshima and Nagasaki: The Physical, Medical, and Social Effects of the Atomic Bombings. Translated by Eisei Ishikawa and D.L. Swain. New York: Basic Books, 1981.

> Translated accounts based on extensive data collected by Japanese officials and scholars.

Hofstadter, Richard. *The American Political Tradition and the Men Who Made It*. New York: Vintage Books, 1989.

> Hofstadter identifies the political tradition of compromise and traces it through U.S. history.

Kaufman, Burton Ira. *The Korean War: Challenges in Crisis, Credibility, and Command*. New York: McGraw-Hill Companies, 1997.

> This book examines the political, diplomatic, and military history of U.S. involvement in the Korean War. Short and well-written, it is accessible to students and provides good background information for further explorations of this topic.

Kennan, George F. *Memoirs, 1925-1963*. 2 vols. Boston: Little, Brown, 1972.

> In the section concerning the cold war period, Kennan discusses the development of the concept of containment. The appendix includes excerpts from Kennan's famous telegram of 22 February 1946.

X [George F. Kennan.] "The Source of Soviet Conduct," *Foreign Affairs*, vol. 25, 1947: pp. 566-582.

> Kennan's explanation of the philosophy of containment is in less hard-line terms than Truman's, and less than Kennan has been blamed for. This article was significant in the development of containment and should be of interest to teachers and to students prepared to do indepth studies of the Truman era.

Koenig, Louis W. *The Chief Executive*. 6th edition. New York: Harcourt Brace College Publishers, 1996.

> This is a study of Presidential leadership and the evolution of Presidential powers. Truman's leadership is reviewed under various topics, such as the A-bomb decision, labor and union disputes, and the courts.

Lafeber, Walter, ed. *The Origins of the Cold War, 1941-1947: A Historical Problem with Interpretations and Documents*. New York: Wiley, 1971.

> This collection of 43 extracts and documents provides an introduction to the basic issues of the cold war, its origin and consequences.

MacArthur, Douglas. *Reminiscences*. Annapolis, MD: Naval Institute Press, 2001.

> This autobiographical memoir has a section titled "Frustration in Korea, 1950-1951."

Marcus, Maeve. *Truman and the Steel Seizure Case: The Limits of Presidential Power*. Durham, NC: Duke University Press, 1994.

> Marcus discusses Truman's seizure of the steel industry in relation to the role of the President and the nature of Presidential power.

McCullough, David. *Truman*. New York: Simon & Schuster, 1992.

> An engaging biography, this work covers the private and public life of Harry Truman. Although of a substantial length, the book is so well-written that it brings to life both Truman and his times.

Miller, Arthur. *The Crucible: A Play in Four Acts*. Rev. ed. New York: Penguin, 1996.

> Miller's play is set in Salem, MA, during the witch hunts. It was seen by critics, however, as a commentary on the "red scare" in the post-World War II period.

O'Neil, William L. *A Better World: Stalinism and the American Intellectuals*. New Brunswick, NJ: Transaction Publishers, 1990.

> O'Neil discusses the struggle among non-Communist leftists and liberals over U.S. relations with the Soviet Union from 1939 through the 1950s in light of the post-World War II red scare.

Oshinsky, David M. *A Conspiracy So Immense: The World of Joe McCarthy*. New York: Free Press, 1983.

> A well-crafted account of the life of Joseph McCarthy and the history of McCarthyism, this work captures the complex nature of McCarthy's ambiguous personality. Oshinsky is determined to explain, but does not excuse, McCarthy's leadership of the red scare of the 1950s.

Pemberton, William E. *Bureaucratic Politics: Executive Reorganization during the Truman Administration*. Columbia: University of Missouri Press, 1979.

> The Department of Defense, the Central Intelligence Agency, the Council of Economic Advisors, the National Security Council, and the Joint Chiefs of Staff were created by Truman reorganization decisions. Pemberton sees reorganization of the executive branch of the federal government as one of Truman's greatest successes.

Potter, David M. *People of Plenty: Economic Abundance and the American Character*. Chicago: University of Chicago Press, 1958.

> Potter sees economic abundance as the shaping experience of U.S. society in the postwar years and advertising as its characteristic institution.

Riesman, David, et al. *The Lonely Crowd: A Study of the Changing American Character*. Abridged and rev. New Haven: Yale University Press, 2001.

> This classic study examines Americans' changing standard for shaping character. Rather than using traditional character models derived from Classical or 18th century traditions, internalized at an early age, Americans looked to each other as standards for behavior. Riesman coined the phrase "other directed" to describe this method of shaping character.

Robinson, Jackie. *I Never Had It Made*. Hopewell, NJ: Ecco Press, 1995.

> This is Robinson's account of breaking the color barrier in major league baseball in 1947.

Schlesinger, Arthur M., Jr. *The Imperial Presidency*. Somerville, NJ: Replica Books, 1998.

> With a focus on the war-making powers of the President, this volume includes a chapter (6) on Truman's decision to send U.S. troops into the Korean War without congressional approval.

Schrecker, Ellen. *Many Are the Crimes: McCarthyism in America.* Boston: Little, Brown, 1998.

> A history of communism and anticommunism in modern American history, this work spans the 1930s to early 1990s. It discusses the key leaders and ideas of the American communist movement, the way American communists attempted to disseminate their political philosophy across the United States, and the various forms of political repression with which these efforts were met.

Smith, John C. *Alger Hiss: The True Story.* New York: Penguin Books, 1977.

> Smith concludes that Hiss was innocent.

Tanenhaus, Sam. *Whittaker Chambers: A Biography.* New York: Random House, 1997.

> This work follows the fascinating life of one of the central figures in the Alger Hiss case of the late 1940s and the rising communist-anticommunist movements in the United States. Written in a lively, engaging style, readers may at times feel like they are reading a spy thriller rather than a history book.

Thomson, David S. *A Pictorial Biography; HST.* New York: Grosset & Dunlop, 1973.

> This volume contains a pictorial view of Truman from his early years in Missouri to his retirement.

To Secure These Rights: Report of the President's Committee on Civil Rights. Washington, DC: U.S. Government Printing Office, 1947.

> This report contains much of the information on which Truman based his civil rights policies.

Truman, Harry S. *Memoirs of Harry S. Truman.* 2 vols. New York: Da Capo Press, 1986-1987.

> Volume I, *Year of Decision*, focuses on the United Nations, Potsdam Hiroshima, and the return to peace. Volume II, *Years of Trial and Hope*, contains Truman's recollections of such episodes as the Marshall Plan, the Berlin airlift, NATO, and the Korean War.

Underhill, Robert. *The Truman Persuasions.* Ames, IA: Iowa State University Press, 1981.

> Underhill examines Truman's speeches and the responses they engendered. Underhill does not consider Truman a great orator, but nevertheless, an effective speaker.

Weinstein, Allen. *Perjury: The Hiss-Chambers Case.* New York: Random House, 1997.

> Weinstein concludes that Hiss stole the documents and that Chambers told the truth about receiving them from Hiss.

Westin, Alan F., ed. *The Anatomy of a Constitutional Law Case: Youngstown Sheet and Tube Company v. Sawyer, The Steel Seizure Decision.* New York: Columbia University Press, 1990.

> This volume is a collection of political and legal documents relating to the steel seizure case, including Truman's seizure speech, Clarence Randall's objection, congressional debates, court transcripts, and judicial opinions.

The Truman Years: 1945-1953
Archival Citations of Documents

1. Luis Alvarez's notes and drawings of the Trinity test blast, the first atomic device, July 16, 1945; General Records of the National Defense Research Committee, Tolman Files; Records of the Office of Scientific Research and Development, Record Group 227; National Archives at College Park, College Park, MD.

2. Memo from Maj. Gen. Leslie Groves to the Chief of Staff of the Army, General of the Army George C. Marshall concerning the delivery of a third atomic bomb for use against Japan, August 10, 1945; MED TS Folder 25Q; Records of the Office of the Chief of Engineers, Record Group 77; National Archives at College Park, College Park, MD.

3. *Duck and Cover*, photograph of a civil defense drill in a school, n.d.; Two pages of the Federal Civil Defense Administration; Manuscript Collection; Harry S. Truman Library, Independence, MO.

4. Message from the Staff of the Commander in Chief Far East to the War Department inquiring about the advisability of allowing Japanese officers to be interrogated by the Russians concerning biological warfare, February 10, 1947; 468, box G2 C. A. P, SWNCC 351; Records of the War Department General and Special Staffs, Record Group 165; National Archives at College Park, College Park, MD.

5. Letter from William Green, President of the American Federation of Labor, to President Harry Truman urging him to veto the Taft-Hartley bill, June 7, 1947; Folder: Labor—H. R. 3020 Taft-Hartley Publications; Subject File, Box 8; Papers of Clark W. Clifford; Harry S. Truman Library, Independence, MO.

6. Pamphlet describing the high cost of living due to inflation for college student veterans, December 1947; attached to cable from Marvin Gerstein to President Truman, January 13, 1948; Official File 190 L, 1948; Papers of Harry S. Truman; Harry S. Truman Library, Independence, MO.

7. Telegram from Commander, Naval Forces Germany to Commander in Chief, North East Atlantic and Mediterranean, the Chief of Naval Operations, and Commander Sixth Fleet documenting the Soviet blockade of Berlin and the relief airlift, June 27, 1948; JCS Chairman File, Admiral Leahy; Box 7; Records of the U. S. Joint Chiefs of Staff, Record Group 218; National Archives at College Park, College Park, MD.

8. Wire story about Senator Robert Taft's opposition to United States' participation in the North Atlantic Treaty Organization (NATO), July 11, 1949; Papers of Frank McNaughton, July 11, 1949, To: Don Bermingham From Frank McNaughton (Washington) Atlantic Pact (NA); Harry S. Truman Library, Independence, MO.

9. Letter from Senator Edwin Johnson to Secretary of State Dean Acheson urging United States' recognition of the People's Republic of China, October 26, 1949; 893.01/10-2649, A-EP; Central Decimal File 1945-1949; General Records of the Department of State, Record Group 59; National Archives at College Park, College Park, MD.

10. Letter from Senator H. Alexander Smith to Secretary of State Dean Acheson opposing United States' recognition of the People's Republic of China, November 5, 1949; 893.01/11-549, CS/M; Central Decimal File 1945-49; General Records of the Department of State, Record Group 59; National Archives at College Park, College Park, MD.

11. Photo of the cover of a report about the Point Four Program, 1950; Folder: Point IV-3, Lloyd files, Pamphlet: Books and Magazines in Point Four; Files of David D. Lloyd; Speech File, Box 20; Papers of Harry S. Truman; Harry S. Truman Library, Independence, MO.

12. Senate Resolution 243, favoring an increased educational program by the United States in combating communism in foreign countries, March 22, 1950; Folder: Point IV-2, Lloyd files, 3-22-50 S. R. 243; Files of David D. Lloyd; Speech File; Box 20; Papers of Harry S. Truman; Harry S. Truman Library, Independence, MO.

13. War Department press release containing Secretary of War Patterson's statement about the transfer of the Manhattan Project to the newly-created Atomic Energy Commission, December 31, 1946; Lillienthal Files; NAF 8828; Records of the Atomic Energy Commission, Record Group 326; National Archives at College Park, College Park, MD.

14. "Everything Unified, Everybody Happy," cartoon concerning the unification of the armed services, Washington *Evening Star*, January 18, 1947; 76-201; Harry S. Truman Library, Independence, MO.

15. Personal message from Chairman of the Joint Chiefs of Staff, General of the Army Omar Bradley to Commander in Chief Far East, General of the Army Douglas MacArthur quoting President Truman's statement relieving MacArthur of command, April 11, 1951; JCS Chairman's File, Bradley, 1949-1953; Records of the U.S. Joint Chiefs of Staff, Record Group 218; National Archives at College Park, College Park, MD.

16. "Who does Truman think he is – the PRESIDENT?" cartoon by Jacob Burck, Chicago *Sun Times*, 1951; Item 58-419-9; Harry S. Truman Library, Independence, MO.

17. The Foreign Assistance Act of 1948 (the Marshall Plan), January 6, 1948; Public Law 472, 80th congress, 2nd Session; General Records of the U.S. Government, Record Group 11; National Archives at College Park, College Park, MD.

18. Cartoon No. 306-PS-49-939; "Making Progress," April 10, 1949, cartoon, *Tampa Tribune*; Records of the U. S. Joint Chiefs of Staff, Record Group 218; National Archives at College Park, College Park, MD.

19. Draft statement of President Truman officially recognizing the State of Israel, May 14, 1948; Subject File; Handwriting of the President; Subject Files; Papers of Charles G. Ross; Harry S. Truman Library, Independence, MO.

20. Military situation map for the State of Israel the day of the first U. N. cease fire order, June 11, 1948; JCS Chairman's File, Admiral Leahy; Records of the U. S. Joint Chiefs of Staff, Record Group 218; National Archives at College Park, College Park, MD.

21. Photograph No. 306-PS-52-565; "Dr. Ralph Bunche at Arab-Israeli armistice talks," 1949; Records of the United States Information Agency, Record Group 306; National Archives at College Park, College Park, MD.

22. Letter from Senator Joseph McCarthy to Senator Millard Tydings, June 3, 1950; Subcommittee on State Department Employee Loyalty Investigation (SEN81A-F8); 81st Congress; Records of the U.S. Senate, Record Group 46; National Archives Building, Washington, DC.

23. Cartoon No. 64-691; "Are You A Communist?" n.d., Providence, RI, *Bulletin*; Harry S. Truman Library, Independence, MO.

24. Denial of the application of a stay of execution in the case of Julius and Ethel Rosenberg—U.S. District Court for the Southern District of New York, December 10, 1952; Case No. 687 and 719, O.T. 1952; Appellate Jurisdiction Case Files, 1792 -; Records of the Supreme Court of the United States, Record Group 267; National Archives Building, Washington, DC.

25. Chart showing comparable newspaper coverage of the Rosenberg case and other espionage subjects early in 1951; Folder 2, p. 160; Case No. 687 and 719, O.T., 1952; Appellate Jurisdiction Case Files, 1792 -;Records of the Supreme Court of the United States, Record Group 267; National Archives Building, Washington, DC.

26. Teletype conference message authorizing full use of Far East Command (FECOM) naval and air forces against the North Korean forces invading South Korea, June 27, 1950; CCS 383.21 Korea, 3-19-45, Sec. 21, NAF 9156 a-b; Records of the U. S. Joint Chiefs of Staff, Record Group 218; National Archives at College Park, College Park, MD.

27. President Truman's proclamation of national emergency, December 16, 1950; Presidential Proclamation 2914; General Records of the U.S. Government, Record Group 11; National Archives at College Park, College Park, MD.

28. Memo from the Joint Chiefs of Staff to the Secretary of Defense discussing the U. S. position regarding an armistice in Korea, March 27, 1951; Folder 5; Confidential Section, CD 092; Secretary of Defense Correspondence; Records of the Office of the Secretary of Defense, Record Group 330; National Archives at College Park, College Park, MD.

29. Photograph No. 64-803; "President Truman campaigning in California," September 24, 1948; Campaign Scrapbook of Harry S. Truman; Paul E. Wolfe, originator; Harry S. Truman Library, Independence, MO.

30. Cartoon No. 64-736; "...and on Two Legs," *Evansville* (IN) *Courier*, November 3, 1948; Harry S. Truman Library, Independence, MO.

31. Suarez letter to Truman about attempted assassination, November 8, 1950; President's Personal File 1N, A; Papers of Harry S. Truman; Harry S. Truman Library, Independence, MO.

32. Letter from G. Raymond Booth, Executive Director, Council for Civic Unity to Dr. Laurence Hewes, Regional Director for the American Council on Race Relations concerning employment conditions for minorities in the Los Angeles area, March 15, 1946; Entry 8, West Coast Materials; Records of the Committee on Fair Employment Practice, Record Group 228; National Archives at College Park, College Park, MD.

33. Executive Order 9981, establishing racial, religious, and national equality for all members of the armed forces, July 26, 1948; General Records of the U.S. Government, Record Group 11; National Archives at College Park, College Park, MD.

34. Photograph No. 306-PS-50-7551; "Jackie Robinson in his Brooklyn Dodgers uniform," 1950; Records of the United States Information Agency, Record Group 306; National Archives at College Park, College Park, MD.

35. "Rests with Other Heroes; Indian Sergeant Is Buried in Dignity, With All Honor," *The Cincinnati Enquirer*, September 5, 1951; Official File, Box 1353, File -OF471B-W; Papers of Harry S. Truman; Harry S. Truman Library, Independence, MO.

36. Photograph No.71-2493; "Carverdale Addition, Negro Housing, Oklahoma City, Oklahoma," 1946; Papers of Philleo Nash; Harry S. Truman Library, Independence, MO.

37. Photograph No. 71-2665; "The Living Room of a Harman Sample Home," May 3, 1949; Papers of David H. Stowe; Harry S. Truman Library, Independence, MO.

38. Advertisement for a Motorola television, February 13, 1950; *Life*; Harry S. Truman Library, Independence, MO.

39. Advertisement of the Lustron Home, 1950; Lustron Home Bulletin of Progress; President's Personal File, OF 1930; Papers of Harry S. Truman; Harry S. Truman Library, Independence, MO.

40. Photograph of an Erikson Oil Products gas station, North Lyndale Minneapolis, December 29, 1954; Civil Case File #5046; USDC for the District of Minnesota, 4ᵗʰ Division–Minneapolis; Records of District Courts of the United States, Record Group 21; National Archives-Central Plains Region.

41. Sound Recording 188-032A; "Musical program in support of the Office of Price Administration," 1946; Records of the Office of Price Administration, Record Group 188; National Archives at College Park, College Park, MD.

42. Sound Recording 208-202; "Winston Churchill's 'Iron Curtain' speech," March 6, 1946; Records of the Office of War Information, Record Group 208; National Archives at College Park, College Park, MD.

43. Sound Recording 200-245; "President Harry S. Truman's, 'Truman Doctrine' speech," March 12, 1947; National Archives Collection of Donated Materials; National Archives at College Park, College Park, MD.

44. Sound Recording 200-WTOP 1084/1085; "Broadcast summary of actor Ronald Reagan's testimony before the House Un-American activities Committee," October 23, 1947; National Archives Collection of Donated Materials; National Archives at College Park, College Park, MD.

45. Sound Recording 200-788; "Secretary of State George C. Marshall's 'Marshall Plan' speech," June 5, 1947; National Archives Collections of Donated Materials; National Archives at College Park, College Park, MD.

46. Sound Recording 200-G-0615; "Broadcast summary of Alger Hiss's testimony before the House Un-American Activities Committee," August 5, 1948; National Archives Collection of Donated Materials; National Archives at College Park, College Park, MD.

47. Sound Recording 330-337C; "Combat in Korea by Wes MacPheron," October 20, 1950; Records of the Office of the Secretary of Defense, Record Group 330; National Archives at College Park, College Park, MD.

About the National Archives:
A Word to Educators

The National Archives and Records Administration (NARA) is responsible for the preservation and use of the permanently valuable records of the federal government. These materials provide evidence of the activities of the government from 1774 to the present in the form of written and printed documents, maps and posters, sound recordings, photographs, films, computer tapes, and other media. These rich archival sources are useful to everyone: federal officials seeking information on past government activities, citizens needing data for use in legal matters, historians, social scientists and public policy planners, environmentalists, historic preservationists, medical researchers, architects and engineers, novelists and playwrights, journalists researching stories, students preparing papers, and persons tracing their ancestry or satisfying their curiosity about particular historical events. These records are useful to you as educators either in preparing your own instructional materials or pursuing your own research.

The National Archives records are organized by the governmental body that created them rather than under a library's subject/author/title categories. There is no Dewey decimal or Library of Congress designation; each departmental bureau or collection of agency's records is assigned a record group number. In lieu of a card catalog, inventories and other finding aids assist the researcher in locating material in records not originally created for research purposes, often consisting of thousands of cubic feet of documentation.

The National Archives is a public institution whose records and research facilities nationwide are open to anyone 14 years of age and over. These facilities are found in the Washington, DC, metropolitan area, in the 11 Presidential libraries, the Nixon Presidential Materials Project, and in 16 regional archives across the nation. Whether you are pursuing broad historical questions or are interested in the history of your family, admittance to the research room at each location requires only that you fill out a simple form stating your name, address, and research interest. A staff member then issues an identification card, which is good for two years.

If you come to do research, you will be offered an initial interview with a reference archivist. You will also be able to talk with archivists who have custody of the records. If you have a clear definition of your questions and have prepared in advance by reading as many of the secondary sources as possible, you will find that these interviews can be very helpful in guiding you to the research material you need.

The best printed source of information about the overall holdings of the National Archives is the *Guide to the National Archives of the United States* (issued in 1974, reprinted in 1988), which is available in university libraries and many public libraries and online at **www.nara.gov**. The *Guide* describes in very general terms the records in the National Archives, gives the background and history of each agency represented by those records, and provides useful information about access to the records. To accommodate users outside of Washington, DC, the regional archives hold microfilm copies of much that is found in Washington. In addition, the regional archives contain records created by field offices of the federal government, including district and federal appellate court records, records of the Bureau of Indian Affairs, National Park Service, Bureau of Land Management, Forest Service, Bureau of the Census, and others. These records are particularly useful for local and regional history studies and in linking local with national historical events.

For more information about the National Archives and its educational and cultural programs, visit NARA's Web site at **www.nara.gov**.

Presidential Libraries

Herbert Hoover Library
210 Parkside Drive
West Branch, IA 52358-0488
319-643-5301

Franklin D. Roosevelt Library
511 Albany Post Road
Hyde Park, NY 12538-1999
914-229-8114

Harry S. Truman Library
500 West U.S. Highway 24
Independence, MO 64050-1798
816-833-1400

Dwight D. Eisenhower Library
200 Southeast Fourth Street
Abilene, KS 67410-2900
785-263-4751

John Fitzgerald Kennedy Library
Columbia Point
Boston, MA 02125-3398
617-929-4500

Lyndon Baines Johnson Library
2313 Red River Street
Austin, TX 78705-5702
512-916-5137

Gerald R. Ford Library
1000 Beal Avenue
Ann Arbor, MI 48109-2114
734-741-2218

Jimmy Carter Library
441 Freedom Parkway
Atlanta, GA 30307-1498
404-331-3942

Ronald Reagan Library
40 Presidential Drive
Simi Valley, CA 93065-0600
805-522-8444/800-410-8354

George Bush Library
1000 George Bush Drive
P.O. Box 10410
College Station, TX 77842-0410
409-260-9552

Clinton Presidential Materials Project
1000 LaHarpe Boulevard
Little Rock, AR 72201
501-254-6866

National Archives Regional Archives

NARA-Northeast Region
380 Trapelo Road
Waltham, MA 02452-6399
781-647-8104

NARA-Northeast Region
10 Conte Drive
Pittsfield, MA 01201-8230
413-445-6885

NARA-Northeast Region
201 Varick Street, 12th Floor
New York, NY 10014-4811
212-337-1300

NARA-Mid Atlantic Region
900 Market Street
Philadelphia, PA 19107-4292
215-597-3000

NARA-Mid Atlantic Region
14700 Townsend Road
Philadelphia, PA 19154-1096
215-671-9027

NARA-Southeast Region
1557 St. Joseph Avenue
East Point, GA 30344-2593
404-763-7474

NARA-Great Lakes Region
7358 South Pulaski Road
Chicago, IL 60629-5898
773-581-7816

NARA-Great Lakes Region
3150 Springboro Road
Dayton, OH 45439-1883
937-225-2852

NARA-Central Plains Region
2312 East Bannister Road
Kansas City, MO 64131-3011
816-926-6272

NARA-Central Plains Region
200 Space Center Drive
Lee's Summit, MO 64064-1182
816-478-7079

NARA-Southwest Region
501 West Felix Street
P.O. Box 6216
Fort Worth, TX 76115-0216
817-334-5525

NARA-Rocky Mountain Region
Denver Federal Center, Building 48
P.O. Box 25307
Denver, CO 80225-0307
303-236-0804

NARA-Pacific Region
24000 Avila Road
P.O. Box 6719
Laguna Niguel, CA 92607-6719
949-360-2641

NARA-Pacific Region
1000 Commodore Drive
San Bruno, CA 94066-2350
650-876-9009

NARA-Pacific Alaska Region
6125 Sand Point Way, NE
Seattle, WA 98115-7999
206-526-6507

NARA-Pacific Alaska Region
654 West Third Avenue
Anchorage, AK 99501-2145
907-271-2443

Reproductions of Documents

Reproductions of the oversized print documents included in these units are available in their original size by special order from Graphic Visions.

An Eye-Witness Account of the Trinity Shot on Monday Morning
at 5:30 AM - 16 July 1945

by

L. W. Alvarez

I was kneeling between the pilot and co-pilot in B-29 No. 384 and observed the explosion through the pilot's window on the left side of the plane. We were about 20 to 25 miles from the site and the cloud cover between us and the ground was approximately 7/10. About 30 seconds before the object was detonated the clouds obscured our vision of the point so that we did not see the initial stages of the ball of fire. I was looking through crossed polaroid glasses directly at the site. My first sensation was one of intense light covering my whole field of vision. This seemed to last for about 1/2 second after which I noted an intense orange red glow through the clouds. Several seconds later it appeared that a second spherical red ball appeared but it is probable that this apparent phenomenon was caused by the motion of the airplane bringing us to a position where we could see through the cloud directly at the ball of fire which had been developing for the past few seconds. This fire ball seemed to have a rough texture with irregular black lines dividing the surface of the sphere into a large number of small patches of reddish orange. This thing disappeared a few seconds later and what seemed to be a third ball of fire appeared again and I am now convinced that this was all the same fire ball which I saw on two separate occasions through a new hole in the undercast.

When this "third ball" disappeared the light intensity dropped considerably and within another 20 seconds or so the cloud started to push up through the undercast. It first appeared as a parachute which was being blown up by a large electric fan. After the hemispherical cap had emerged through the cloud layer one could see a cloud of smoke about 1/3 the diameter of the "parachute" connecting the bottom of the hemisphere with the undercast. This had very much the appearance of a large mushroom. The hemispherical structure was creased with "longitude lines" running from the pole to the equator. In another minute the equatorial region had partially caught up with the poles giving a flattened out appearance to the top of the structure. In the next few minutes the symmetry of the structure was broken up by the wind currents at various altitudes so the shape of the cloud cannot be described in any geometrical manner. In about 8 minutes the top of the cloud was at approximately 40,000 feet as close as I could estimate from our altitude at 24,000 feet and this seemed to be the maximum altitude attained by the cloud. I did not feel the shock wave hit the plane but the pilot felt the reaction on the rudder through the rudder pedals. Some of the other passengers in the plane noted a rather small shock at the time but it was not apparent to me.

I am attaching two sketches of the cloud which I made at the times noted. Mr. Glenn Fowler had made several sketches earlier in the development.

Luis W. Alvarez

Document 1a. Alvarez's notes and drawings of the first atomic explosion, July 16, 1945. [National Archives]

estimated 40,000 ft.

Looking toward 80°
(Plane flying 170°)

5:38 AM
(8 minutes after detonation)

approximate plane altitude = 24,000 ft above sea level.

undercast

CLASSIFICATION CANCELLED
OR CHANGED TO Unclassified
BY AUTHORITY OF H. 7. Carroll
BY B. Wuy DATE 1-27-67

SECRET

Alvarez

Document 1b. Alvarez's notes and drawings of the
first atomic explosion, July 16, 1945. [National Archives]

Document 1c. Alvarez's notes and drawings of the first atomic explosion, July 16, 1945. [National Archives]

WAR DEPARTMENT

WASHINGTON

10 August 1945.

MEMORANDUM TO: Chief of Staff.

The next bomb of the implosion type had been scheduled to be ready for delivery on the target on the first good weather after 24 August 1945. We have gained 4 days in manufacture and expect to ship from New Mexico on 12 or 13 August the final components. Providing there are no unforeseen difficulties in manufacture, in transportation to the theatre or after arrival in the theatre, the bomb should be ready for delivery on the first suitable weather after 17 or 18 August.

L. R. GROVES,
Major General, USA.

8/10/45

It is not to be released on Japan without express authority from the President.

REGRADED UNCLASSIFIED
ORDER SEC ARMY BY TAG PER 41602

Document 2. Groves' memo to Chief of Staff regarding third atomic bomb, August 10, 1945. [National Archives]

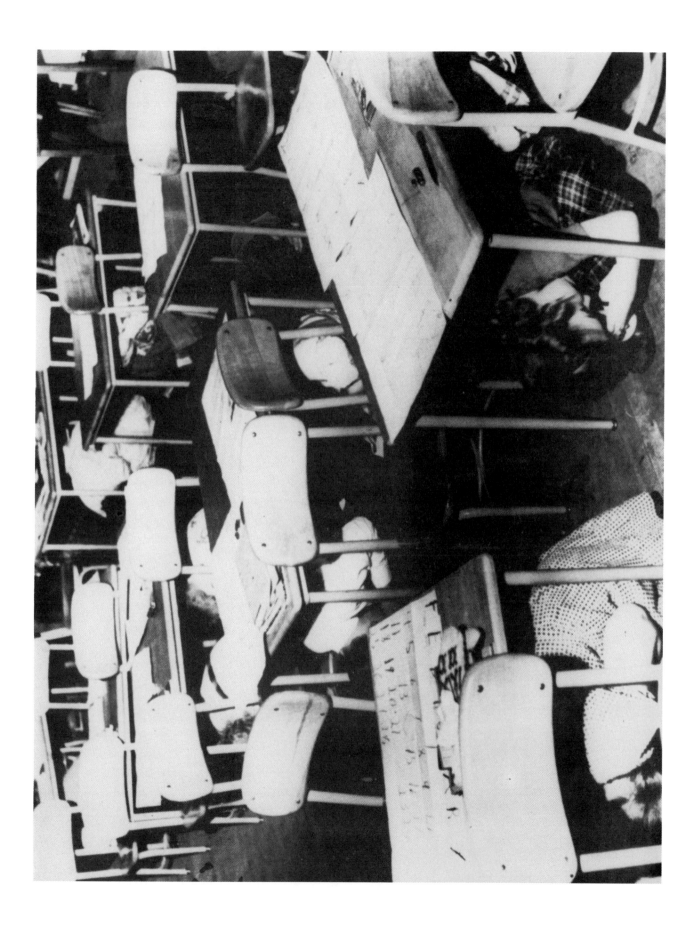

Document 3. Photograph of a civil defense drill, n.d. [National Archives]

ENCLOSURE

From: CINCFE Tokyo Japan

To: War Department for WDCSA

Nr: C-69946   10 February 1947

Prosecutor for USSR at IMTFE requests permission to interrogate former Japanese General Ishii, Colonel Kikughi, and Colonel Ota, all formerly connected with bacteriological warfare research and experiments at Pingfan laboratory near Harbin, Manchuria. Request based on information alleged to have been obtained from unidentified prisoners of war who stated that experiments authorized and conducted by above 3 Japanese resulted in deaths of 2,000 Chinese and Manchurians. Russians present request on their assumption that supplementary war crimes trials will be authorized by United States, but also admit interest in mass production of typhus and cholera bacteria and typhus bearing fleas at Pingfan said to have been described by prisoners of war to them.

Opinion here that Russians not likely to obtain information from Japanese not already known to United States and that United States might get some additional information from Russian line of questioning in monitored interrogations. In compliance with paragraphs 3 E and 5 of urad WX 95147, 24 July 1946 (Appendix) request decision as to whether to permit USSR to conduct these interrogations.

End.

CM-IN 1604 (10 Feb 47)

Document 4a. Commander in Chief Far East memo to War Department regarding interrogation of Japanese generals, February 10, 1947. [National Archives]

A P P E N D I X

MESSAGE TO SCAP

Following Radio in two parts.

PART I

Re URAD 69946 of 10 February. Subject to following con-
ditions permission granted for ** SCAP controlled* Soviet interrogation General
Ishii, Colonels Kikuchi and Ota topic Biological Warfare.

    <u>a.</u> Colonels Kikuchi and Ota to be interviewed by the
most competent U. S. personnel available in Japan.

    <u>b.</u> If any information brought out by preliminary
interrogation considered of sufficient importance that
divulgence to Soviets should not be permitted, Kikuchi
and Ota are to be instructed not to reveal such information
to Soviets.

    <u>c.</u> If in your opinion no officer on your staff competent
to determine whether such vital BW info might be revealed,
a transcript of the preliminary U. S. interrogation should
be forwarded by air to War Department.

    <u>d.</u> Prior to interview by Soviets the Japanese BW
experts should be instructed to make no mention of U. S.
interview on this subject.

PART II

Since there is no clear cut war crime interest by the
Soviets in acts allegedly committed by the Japanese against
the Chinese, permission for the interrogation should not be
granted on that basis, but rather as an amiable gesture toward
a friendly government. It should be made clear to the Soviets
that the permission granted in this instance does not create a
precedent for future requests, which shall be considered on
their individual merits.

* P & O change

Document 4b. Commander in Chief Far East memo to War Department regarding
interrogation of Japanese generals, February 10, 1947. [National Archives]

AMERICAN FEDERATION OF LABOR

Executive Council
President, WILLIAM GREEN
Secretary-Treasurer, GEORGE MEANY
A. F. of L. Building, Washington, D. C.

First Vice-President, WILLIAM L. HUTCHESON,
Carpenters' Bldg., Indianapolis, Ind.
Second Vice-President, MATTHEW WOLL,
570 Lexington Ave., New York, N. Y.
Third Vice-President, JOSEPH N. WEBER,
621 Alta Drive, Beverly Hills, Los Angeles, Calif.
Fourth Vice-President, G. M. BUGNIAZET,
1200 Fifteenth St., N. W., Washington, D. C.
Fifth Vice-President, GEO. M. HARRISON,
Railway Clerks' Bldg., Cincinnati, O.
Sixth Vice-President, DANIEL J. TOBIN,
222 East Michigan St., Indianapolis, Ind.

Seventh Vice-President, HARRY C. BATES,
815 Fifteenth St., N. W., Washington, D. C.
Eighth Vice-President, W. D. MAHON,
Post Office Box 611, Inglewood, Fla.
Ninth Vice-President, FELIX H. KNIGHT,
4965 Westwood Road, Kansas City 2, Mo.
Tenth Vice-President, W. C. BIRTHRIGHT,
Delaware at Twelfth Street, Indianapolis, Ind.
Eleventh Vice-President, W. C. DOHERTY,
406 A. F. of L. Bldg., Washington, D. C.
Twelfth Vice-President, DAVID DUBINSKY,
1710 Broadway, New York, N. Y.
Thirteenth Vice-President, JOHN L. LEWIS,
United Mine Workers' Bldg., Washington, D. C.

LONG DISTANCE TELEPHONE NATIONAL 3870-1-2-3-4
CABLE ADDRESS AFEL.

Washington 1, D. C. June 7, 1947.

Honorable Harry S. Truman,
President of the United States,
The White House, Washington, D.C.

Dear Mr. President,

I respectfully and earnestly request you to veto the Taft-Hartley anti-labor bill. I am confident that through your veto of this highly objectionable anti-labor bill you will render a great public service.

In making this request, I am endeavoring to detach myself from the official position I occupy and to look at the real effect upon the economic life of the nation if the Taft-Hartley Bill becomes law, from the standpoint of an American citizen.

The experience which I have gained through a close contact with management-labor relations over a long and extended period of time, convinces me that the operation of a law such as the Taft-Hartley Bill would promote class hatred, industrial chaos, unsound management-labor relations, and the creation of a political controversy which will run indefinitely.

Aside from the attack on the fundamentals of personal freedom which working men and women cherish as a common heritage the anti-labor bill referred to in this communication would render unions weak and impotent, would impose on labor a form of involuntary servitude, create a highly objectionable bureau-cracy, and provide methods by which labor-hating employers could destroy unions through the instutition of civil damage suits.

Permit me to set forth in chronological order the principal reasons for the submission of this request that you veto the Taft-Hartley Bill.

First, the Taft-Hartley Bill is a more vicious and objectionable bill than the Case Bill, which you vetoed on June 11, 1946. The reasons you assigned for your veto of the Case Bill apply with increasing emphasis to the Taft-Hartley Bill. The Taft-Hartley Bill is much more objectionable and destructive of the rights of Labor than the Case Bill.

Second, you recommended in the message you sent to Congress on January 6, 1947, that a committee truly representative of management, labor and the public be authorized and appointed, to investigate management-labor relations and industrial problems in order to determine what character and kind of labor legislation, if any, should be acted upon by Congress. This called for an investigation first, and the enactment of legislation second. Instead Congress ignored your recommendation, refused to comply with it, and passed anti-labor legislation before even considering the appointment of a committee to investigate management-labor relations.

Third, under the provisions of the anti-labor Taft-Hartley Bill labor unions are forbidden to use any of their funds for the purpose of acquainting the voters through their official publications and printed pamphlets, with the records made by Members of Congress or the votes cast by said Members of Congress in favor of or in opposition to legislation in which working men and women are deeply interested. That means a union, created by working men and women, can not function as a union agency for the dissemination of information to the members of said unions and their friends as to how Members of Congress voted on legislation in which working men, not only as workers but as American citizens, are deeply interested. For this reason alone the Taft-Hartley Bill should be vetoed.

Fourth. This anti-labor Taft-Hartley Bill should be vetoed for political reasons. It represents an attack upon the principles of the economic as well as social policies pursued by the Democratic administration for more than a decade. It emasculates the Wagner Labor Relations Act which is regarded as the Magna Carta of Labor and which was passed as a part of the economic policy of the Democratic Party. It restores government by injunction in a large way, at least. It confers upon employers the right to institute damage suits against unions. That means that employers who wish to destroy unions can employ traitorous individuals who would incite workers to violate agreements in order to create a basis for damage suits against the union's treasury. These traitorous individuals, acting for employers who hate unions and who wish to destroy them, can incite the workers and influence them to engage in unauthorized strikes for the correction of real or fancied wrongs. The power to accomplish this purpose is conferred upon union-hating employers by the provisions of the Taft-Hartley Bill.

Mr. President, you will render a great service to our country as well as to Labor if you will veto the Taft-Hartley Bill when it is presented to you for executive action. I appeal to you in the name and in behalf of the millions of working men and women identified with the American Federation of Labor to do so.

Very sincerely yours,

President,
American Federation of Labor.

Y

Document 5b. Green's letter to Truman about the Taft-Hartley Act,
June 7, 1947 (Harry S. Truman Presidential Library). [National Archives]

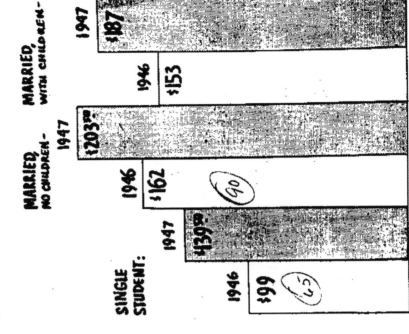

HOW MUCH DOES IT COST
A STUDENT TO LIVE?

MARRIED,
WITH CHILDREN—

1947 $187

1946 $153

MARRIED,
NO CHILDREN—

1947 $203⁹⁹

1946 $162   (40)

SINGLE
STUDENT:

1947 $139⁹⁹

1946 $99   (5)

AVERAGE MONTHLY COST OF LIVING BASED ON CAMPUS SURVEYS
AT UNIVERSITY OF MICHIGAN, NOV. '46 & NOV. '47.

OPERATION SUBSISTENCE
MICHIGAN
REPORT ON:

COST OF
LIVING

OF
STUDENT
VETERANS
at University of Michigan

PUBLISHED DEC. 1947 BY
AMERICAN VETERANS COMMITTEE,
UNIVERSITY OF MICHIGAN CHAPTER
NATIONAL NO. 67.

Document 6a. Pamphlet about the cost of living of student veterans,
December 1947 (Harry S. Truman Presidential Library). [National Archives]

ARE STUDENT VETS MEETING LIVING COSTS ON GI BILL SUBSISTENCE ALLOWANCES?

100% SAY NO

GI SUBSISTENCE ALLOWANCES cover less than one half of the average monthly living costs of vet students, single or married. Spiralling living costs, pressure to make up for lost school years, and an interest in doing serious college work conspire to make part-time employment an increasingly inadequate solution to a growing problem.

FROM WHAT SOURCES DO THEY MAKE UP THE DEFICIT?

SINGLE STUDENTS MAKE UP THE DEFICIT BY:

Source	%
WITHDRAWING SAVINGS	83%
GIFTS FROM HOME	56%
CASHING WAR BONDS	39%
WORKING	28%
LOANS	21%

MARRIED STUDENTS WITHOUT CHILDREN DEPEND ON:

Source	%
WITHDRAWING SAVINGS	80%
WIFE'S EMPLOYMENT	78%
GIFTS FROM HOME	44%
CASHING WAR BONDS	37%
WORKING	31%
LOANS	29%

MARRIED STUDENTS WITH CHILDREN DEPEND ON:

Source	%
WITHDRAWING SAVINGS	97%
CASHING WAR BONDS	62%
WORKING	50%
GIFTS FROM HOME	46%
LOANS	29%
WIFE'S EMPLOYMENT	9%

DO STUDENT VETS DEPEND on the GI BILL FOR THEIR COLLEGE TRAINING?

YES

	%
UNMARRIED	63%
MARRIED, NO CHILDREN	86%
MARRIED WITH CHILDREN	97%

VET STUDENTS SAY that GI Bill Subsistence is like the old joke about a wife: you can't live with them but you can't live without them. A majority of all students interviewed testified that without the GI Bill they wouldn't be in college at all, and this majority included 97 per cent of all vet students with families.

But getting along as a student vet is no joke. Students are drawing heavily on savings, banking on the folks back home, the wife and -- in many cases -- working part-time. Married students are depleting savings which should be preserved to meet emergency and expected needs of a growing family.

Document 6b. Pamphlet about the cost of living of student veterans, December 1947 (Harry S. Truman Presidential Library). [National Archives]

WHAT DOES IT ALL ADD UP TO?

STUDENT VETERANS AREN'T HAVING AN EASY TIME OF IT, BUT NEITHER ARE THEY ASKING THE GOVERNMENT TO UNDERWRITE THEIR ENTIRE LIVING COSTS.

A glance at the charts at the left makes it clear that student veterans ask not for a real increase, but only that Congress re-adjust the subsistence allowance to meet the rise in living costs since 1945.

ACCELERATING LIVING COSTS have already forced thousands of students to give up their hopes for college training. As savings and war bonds continue to dwindle, as family respon-sibilities increase, the total number of abandoned plans will continue to pile up.

VETS SET SCHOLARSHIP RECORDS

On the campus student veterans have set the pace for seriousness of purpose and high scholarship. They have justified the confi-dence of the Congress. They have dramatized the practical effectiveness of democratic adult education.

INFLATION DEMANDS READJUSTMENT

IT WILL TAKE MORE THAN A PAT ON THE BACK to help the student veteran keep up his good record. It will take a realistic look at what has happened to the American Dollar in the past four years, and how it has slashed into the GI subsistence check.

WHAT DO STUDENT VETS WANT?

FOR UNMARRIED STUDENTS:

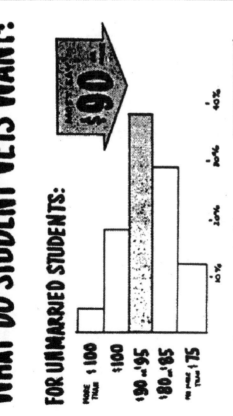

MORE THAN $100
$100
$90 to $95
$80 to $85
LESS THAN $75

MOST SAY $90

10%   20%   30%   40%

FOR MARRIED STUDENTS:

$150 to $200
$135 to $150
$120 to $130
$110 to $115
$95 to $105

MOST SAY $125

10%   20%   30%   40%

ADDITIONAL ALLOTMENT, PER CHILD:

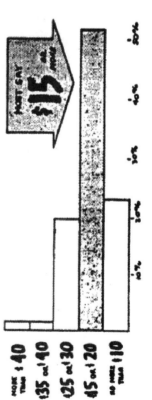

MORE THAN $40
$35 to $40
$25 to $30
$15 to $20
NO MORE THAN $10

MOST SAY $15

10%   20%   30%   40%

Document 6c. Pamphlet about the cost of living of student veterans, December 1947 (Harry S. Truman Presidential Library). [National Archives]

WHERE DOES THE MONEY GO?

UNMARRIED STUDENTS SPEND IT ON:

MARRIED STUDENTS WITHOUT KIDS SPEND IT ON: $203.50

MARRIED STUDENTS WITH KIDS SPEND IT ON: $187.00

$139.50

Unmarried students:
- CLOTHING, INSURANCE, LAUNDRY, CLEANING, TRANSPORTATION, Etc
- RENT $22.75
- FOOD $58.00

Married students without kids:
- CLOTHING, INSURANCE, LAUNDRY, CLEANING, TRANSPORTATION, ETC.
- RENT $50.50
- FOOD $67.75

Married students with kids:
- CLOTHING, INSURANCE, LAUNDRY, TRANSPORTATION, ETC
- RENT $42.50
- FOOD $80.25

(Scale markers: $200, $175, $150, $125, $100, $75, $50, $25)

OPERATION SUBSISTENCE is a nation-wide student veteran movement organized to make Congress and the Nation aware of the impact of inflation upon student veterans.

University of Michigan vets -- participating in a state-wide cost-of-living survey sponsored by OPERATION SUBSISTENCE MICHIGAN -- won the counsel and aid of faculty members and students experienced in scientific survey methods, methods which report on a true cross-section of student-vet population.

THE COLD FIGURES gathered in the 1946 and 1947 surveys show that the student vet faces more problems than he sees in his text books. No one, vet or non-vet has escaped the spiralling cost of living.

Married vets are forced to depend heavily upon their wives' earnings. Married vets with children have no such recourse, are forced to sharply curtail living standards, make heavy withdrawls on savings and War Bonds. The following pages present a more detailed analysis of the problems vet students face, and how they are met.

Document 6d. Pamphlet about the cost of living of student veterans, December 1947 (Harry S. Truman Presidential Library). [National Archives]

| NAVY DEPARTMENT

DRAFTED	EXTENSION NUMBER	ADDRESSEES	PRECEDENCE
		ASTERISK (*) MAILGRAM ADDRESSEE	

FROM COMNAVFORGER Adm. Schuirmann

RELEASED BY

DATE 27 JUNE 1948

TOR CODE ROOM 2140/26

DECODED BY MONYPENY

TYPED BY CONNORS

ROUTED BY WALLS

FOR ACTION

CINCNELM
ADM CONNOLY

PRIORITY ROUTINE
DEFERRED

INFORMATION

C N O - ADM DENFELD
COMSIXTH TASKFLEET
ADM SHERMAN

PRIORITY
ROUTINE
DEFERRED

UNLESS OTHERWISE INDICATED THIS DISPATCH WILL BE TRANSMITTED WITH DEFERRED PRECEDENCE

PAGE 1 OF 2   261030Z   NCR 7470

ORIGINATOR FILL IN DATE AND TIME | DATE | TIME | GCT

ON OUTGOING DISPATCHES PLEASE LEAVE ABOUT ONE INCH CLEAR SPACE BEFORE BEGINNING TEXT

REF NO CC4890 ACTION TO CINCNELM INFO TO CNO: COMSIXTHTASKFLT FROM COMNAVFORGER.

THIS IS MY 261030Z.

AS OF 1000Z JUNE 26 ALL RAIL TRAFFIC BETWEEN BERLIN AND WESTERN ZONE REMAINS SUSPENDED. INCOMING AUTOMOBILE TRAFFIC SUSPENDED OUTGOING TRAFFIC PERMITTED. PLANES OPERATING NORMALLY. SOVIET HAVE FORBIDDEN FOOD SHIPMENTS FROM SOVIET ZONE TO BERLIN WESTERN SECTORS. SUPPLY AMERICAN COMMUNITY BY AIR STARTED JUNE 23. BASED ON FIRST 3 DAYS OPERATION AVERAGE DAILY INCOMING LIFT 75 TONS AVERAGE DAILY INCOMING FLIGHTS 32. ESTIMATED SUPPLIES ON HAND FOOD FOR GERMAN POPULATION WESTERN SECTORS ABOUT 15 DAYS, COAL FOR WESTERN SECTOR ELECTRIC POWER PLANTS 2 TO 3 WEEKS, COAL AND (POL) PRODUCTS FOR OCCUPATION FORCES 3 MONTHS UNLESS PART DIVERTED TO SUPPLY GERMAN POPULATION, GENERAL MEDICAL SUPPLIES 2 MONTHS. WESTERN SECTOR POWER PLANTS

SECRET

DECLASSIFIED BY:
JCS DECLASSIFICATION BRANCH
DATE 6 FEB 1974

MAY BE HANDLED AS CORRESPONDENCE OF SAME CLASSIFICATION

261030Z

OPNAV 19-67

Document 7a. Telegram about the Berlin blockade and airlift, June 27, 1948. [National Archives]

CAN SUPPLY ABOUT 50% OF CURRENT NORMALLY USED. BOTH WESTERN
POWERS AND SOVIET HAVE STARTED CONVERSION OF CURRENCY IN THEIR
SECTORS. SOVIET HAVE FORBIDDEN POSSESSION OF WESTERN MARK
BY BERLIN POPULATION. CIRCULATION SOVIET MARK IN WESTERN
SECTORS IS PERMITTED. CITY IS QUIET.

SIGNED SCHUIRMANN.

OPO3(35)...COG...

SECDEF...SECNAV...OPOO6...20-2...A2...NAVAIDE...20...ARMY(ID)...

Document 7b. Telegram about the Berlin blockade and airlift, June 27, 1948. [National Archives]

RUSH   RUSH   RUSH

July 11, 1949

To: Don Bermingham

From: Frank McNaughton (Washington)

Atlantic Pact (NA)

Today, Bob Taft of Ohio teed off against, repeat against, ratification

of the pact in one of the best speeches of the whole debate. (For full roundup

on Taft see AP wire.)

"I cannot", said Taft, "vote in favor of ratifying the North Atlantic

tre aty because I think it carries with it an x obligation to assist in arming

at our e xpense the nations of Western Europe, because with that obligation I

believe it will promote war in the world rather than peace, and because I think

that with the arms plan it is wholly contrary to the spirit of the obligations we

assumed in the United Nations charter. I would vote for the pact if a reservation

were adopted denying any legal or moral obligation to provide arms."

We are not repeating here all of Taft's arguments which you will find

fully summarized in your AP dispatches. At one point Taft said:

"Obviously, any help we give one of these nations today may

be used later for aggressive purposes, against Russia or its satellites, or neutrals, or members of the Pact, or it may even be used against us when we try to ~~fulfill~~ fulfill our obligation to other members of the pact. Except for the warning conveyed to Soviet Russia, this treaty does not bear the slightest resemblance to the Monroe Doctrine".

It is now likely that a vote may be deferred until late in the week because Taft's speech is certainly a shot in the arm to the opposition, although it m ay not finally line up many additional votes against ratification.

68   October 26, 1949

EDWIN C. JOHNSON, COLO., CHAIRMAN
ERNEST W. MC FARLAND, ARIZ.   CHARLES W. TOBEY, N. H.
WARREN G. MAGNUSON, WASH.   CLYDE M. REED, KANS.
FRANK J. MYERS, PA.   OWEN BREWSTER, MAINE
BRIEN MC MAHON, CONN.   HOMER E. CAPEHART, IND.
HERBERT R. O'CONOR, MD.   JOHN W. BRICKER, OHIO
LYNDON B. JOHNSON, TEX.
ESTES KEFAUVER, TENN.

EDWARD S. JARRETT, CLERK

United States Senate

COMMITTEE ON
INTERSTATE AND FOREIGN COMMERCE

Hon. Dean Acheson
Secretary of State
Washington, D. C.

My dear Secretary Acheson:

I have watched with great interest the developments in China and the sincere efforts of our State Department to react in an intelligent, realistic and constructive manner to that dynamic situation.

I have sincerely believed that the former policy of military and other support for the Nationalist Government of Chiang Kai Shek has been in error since available evidence has demonstrated the completely corrupt and irresponsible character of that government.

It seems to me we must recognize that after centuries of cruel military and tyrannical oppression, the mass of Chinese people have lost hope and are now turning to a government which paints pretty pictures and might possibly give them needed social and economic change and the peace they want so badly.

It is reported to me that our missionaries whose experience in China is many generations old are unanimously of the opinion that the new government in China should be promptly recognized. It is their experience that this government might possibly cooperate in a forthright manner and might possibly create conditions which will mean progress in their work.

I am informed by various shipping lines, cotton exporters, and other American businessmen who have transacted business in China for 40 years that the new government is eager to conduct normal trade with American businessmen. More than this, these businessmen are fearful that a continued policy of non-recognition may lose to us the Chinese market for many years. Since the British Government and British businessmen plan to make this market the exclusive province of British shipping, it seems desirable that our State Department should promptly take those steps which would protect the interests of American business in China.

217065

EP/(class. phot made)
4/m

OFFICE OF
INTERNATIONAL TRADE POLICY

NOV 25 1949

DEPARTMENT OF STATE

Document 9a. Senator Johnson's letter to Dean Acheson supporting recognition of the People's Republic of China, October 26, 1949. [National Archives]

Hon. Dean Acheson
10/25/49

I am firmly convinced that the best way to win the friendship of the Chinese people and to influence the general course of the development of the new Chinese Government away from Russia is to engage in business and diplomatic relationships with them on the normal American basis of free enterprise and mutual benefit. This is one calculated risk which I favor taking now. What I fear most is that for lack of courage to face realities we may drive China even farther into the arms of Russia.

The outmoded nineteenth century notion that military power can forever hold the Asiatic peoples in economic and political subservience should no longer serve as a basis for American policy.

Obviously, the masses in India, Burma, Indonesia, Siam and Indo-China are watching with deep interest the development of our policy with respect to the heroic efforts of their neighbor for independence and well-being.

They deserve their independence; we need their friendship. They deserve the chance for development; we and the rest of the world need an enlightened neighbor. They need the products of our industries; we need their markets.

Please be assured that I shall continue to follow the growth of our policy in Asia with hope and intense interest.

Sincerely yours,

Ed Johnson

ECJ/jsk

Document 9b. Senator Johnson's letter to Dean Acheson supporting recognition
of the People's Republic of China, October 26, 1949. [National Archives]

United States Senate

COMMITTEE ON FOREIGN RELATIONS

November 5, 1949

89

Dear Dean:

I had hoped to see you before this to have a chance
to talk to you personally about my experience in the Far East.
I see by the papers that you are leaving at once for Paris for
the conference with the British and French, and therefore there
will be no opportunity for me to see you before you go. I
realize the pressure you are under and want to send you my very
best wishes as you undertake these important deliberations.

There are two matters I wanted particularly to
emphasize in my talk with you, and I can state them in this letter,
with the hope that I can elaborate my reasons at a later date:

(1) I am strongly of the conviction that we should not
recognize the Chinese communist government at this time, and
furthermore I hope it will be possible for you with your eloquence
and diplomacy to persuade the British not to do so. From con-
versations with the British authorities in Hong Kong, I was
convinced that they were thinking exclusively in terms of (a) defense
of Hong Kong, and at any cost retaining it in British possession,
and (b) the pressure of their commercial interests in Shanghai and
Hong Kong to recognize the Commies, so that traditional British
trade can go on as before.

I was also impressed, however, with the statements
of the British representatives that they felt whatever stand was
taken, should be taken with the United States and not apart from
the United States. I feel, therefore, that our strong stand against
recognition would have a weighty effect upon the British position.
In any event, however, I urge that we do not make the mistake, as I

230940

Document 10a. Senator Smith's letter to Dean Acheson opposing recognition
of the People's Republic of China, November 5, 1949. [National Archives]

see it, of recognizing the present Chinese communist government. Many things can happen in the next few months.

(2) The second important conviction that came to me from my trip was that under no conditions should we let Formosa fall into the hands of the Chinese communists or under the domination of Russia. This of course presents a very difficult question, and it is problematical whether the Nationalist government could defend Formosa without further aid from us. From the standpoint of our own national security, however, I was convinced from my visit on the ground and getting the feel of our strategical island bases that the occupation of Formosa by hostile forces would definitely threaten our security. I did not arrive at this conclusion from any strategical knowledge of my own, which I make no claim to, but from the insistence of our military and naval forces wherever I went that this was a very dangerous issue and that we could not afford to pass it up.

There have been many suggested formulas to handle this delicate matter and I am confident that we can find one on which we can all agree, and which will be in the best interests of the Taiwans themselves. I want to have the opportunity to review these possibilities with you and with our Foreign Relations and Armed Services Committees.

I am sending this line to you at this time because I feel that these matters are urgent and all of us who have responsibility for our foreign policy should be working together and in complete understanding.

With kindest personal regards and best wishes for the success of your trip, I remain

Always cordially yours,

H. Alexander Smith

Honorable Dean Acheson
Secretary of State
Department of State
Washington, D.C.

HAS:W

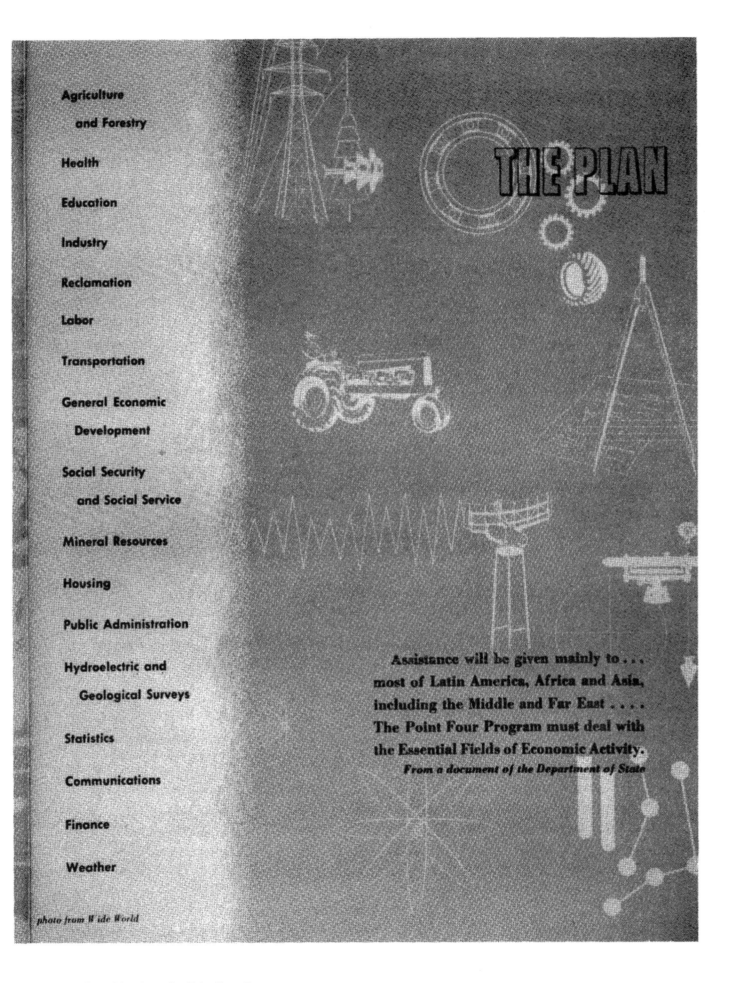

Agriculture
    and Forestry

Health

Education

Industry

Reclamation

Labor

Transportation

General Economic
    Development

Social Security
    and Social Service

Mineral Resources

Housing

Public Administration

Hydroelectric and
    Geological Surveys

Statistics

Communications

Finance

Weather

photo from Wide World

THE PLAN

Assistance will be given mainly to . . .
most of Latin America, Africa and Asia,
including the Middle and Far East . . . .
The Point Four Program must deal with
the Essential Fields of Economic Activity.

From a document of the Department of State

Document 11. Pamphlet about the Point Four Program,
1950 (Harry S. Truman Presidential Library). [National Archives]

81st CONGRESS
2d SESSION

S. RES. 243

IN THE SENATE OF THE UNITED STATES

MARCH 22 (legislative day, MARCH 8), 1950

Mr. BENTON (for himself, Mr. DOUGLAS, Mr. FLANDERS, Mr. FULBRIGHT, Mr.
GRAHAM, Mr. HENDRICKSON, Mr. LEHMAN, Mr. McMAHON, Mr. MORSE,
Mr. MUNDT, Mrs. SMITH of Maine, Mr. SPARKMAN, and Mr. TOBEY) sub-
mitted the following resolution; which was referred to the Committee on
Foreign Relations

RESOLUTION

Whereas the struggle now raging between freedom and communism is a contest for the minds and loyalties of men:
and

Whereas in such a struggle force and the threat of force do not
change men's minds or win their loyalties; and

Whereas the real methods of Communist aggression are incessant
and skillful propaganda designed to prepare the way for
political infiltration, for sabotage, and for the consolidation
of power by suppression and terror; and

Whereas these tactics have poisoned and continue to poison the
minds of hundreds of millions throughout the world; and

Whereas we have learned that such Communist methods cannot
be beaten back by arms and dollars alone but require world-

wide offensive in behalf of the ideas which express our democratic principles and aspirations: Therefore be it

1   *Resolved,* That the United States should initiate and

2 vigorously prosecute a greatly expanded program of informa-

3 tion and education among all the peoples of the world to

4 the full extent that they can be reached—with a view to

5 closing the mental gulf that separates the United States from

6 other peoples and that now blockades the universal hope

7 for freedom and peace; be it further

8   *Resolved,* That it is the sense of the Senate that any

9 such program should encompass, among other things—

10   (1) maintenance, through the United Nations and

11 through our own diplomacy, of a steady and steadily

12 increasing pressure in behalf of world-wide freedom of

13 information;

14   (2) acceleration of the work of the United Nations

15 Educational, Scientific, and Cultural Organization to the

16 point where, with effective leadership, it has a chance

17 to make a significant, perhaps decisive, contribution to

18 peace;

19   (3) development of the activities of the Offices of

20 International Information and Educational Exchange in

21 the Department of State, in the following ways among

22 many others—

23   (a) preparation and execution of a compre-

hensive world-wide program to exhibit documentary and educational motion pictures designed to explain the democratic principles and ideals which underlie our foreign policy;

(b) significant and immediate expansion of our program for bringing foreign students to the United States;

(c) creation of a world broadcasting network capable of broadcasting on long wave, short wave, or medium wave, with an ultimate goal of reaching virtually every radio set in the world;

(d) use of any and all possible means to reach people who are shut off from the free world by censorship and suppression;

(4) promotion of democratic education abroad, notably in the occupied areas of Germany and Japan;

(5) convening of a conference of non-Communist nations now conducting international information programs, with a view to reaching a better understanding on common themes and on greatly increasing the effectiveness of the projection of such themes;

(6) encouragement of the establishment of a nongovernmental agency to help inspire and guide the efforts of the millions of private American citizens who might use their talents and resources and contacts over-

1   seas in furtherance of the programs and objectives of this

2   resolution.

3   and be it further

4   *Resolved,* That it is the sense of the Senate that the

5   international propagation of the democratic creed be made

6   an instrument of supreme national policy—by the develop-

7   ment of a Marshall plan in the field of ideas.

81ST CONGRESS
2D SESSION

S. RES. 243

RESOLUTION

Favoring an increased educational program by the United States in combating communism in foreign countries.

By Mr. BENTON, Mr. DOUGLAS, Mr. FLANDERS, Mr. FULBRIGHT, Mr. GRAHAM, Mr. HEN-DRICKSON, Mr. LEHMAN, Mr. McMAHON, Mr. MORSE, Mr. MUNDT, Mrs. SMITH of Maine, Mr. SPARKMAN, and Mr. TOBEY

MARCH 22 (legislative day, MARCH 8), 1950
Referred to the Committee on Foreign Relations

IMMEDIATE   **RELEASE**

WAR DEPARTMENT
PUBLIC RELATIONS DIVISION
PRESS SECTION
TEL. RE 6700
BRS. 2528 AND 4860

December 31, 1946

STATEMENT OF SECRETARY OF WAR PATTERSON
ON TRANSFER OF MANHATTAN DISTRICT

With the transfer of responsibility for the Nation's atomic energy program
from the War Department to the U. S. Atomic Energy Commission, we will have
carried out the long range plans of President Roosevelt, President Truman, Secretary Stimson, and General Marshall, who months before Hiroshima clearly
recognized that Congress should create an independent agency of the government
to carry on this vital work.

The War Department has consistently supported the principle of civilian
control of atomic energy in its broad aspects, and we look forward to a relationship with the Atomic Energy Commission that will be of mutual advantage. I want
to pledge to Chairman Lilienthal, Doctor Bacher, Mr. Pike, Mr. Strauss, and Mr.
Waymack the continuing wholehearted cooperation and support of the War Department.

The Commission is taking over a well organized and efficient activity.
General Groves has maintained the Manhattan District in a state of readiness for
transfer to the Commission, and he has directed its operations with an efficiency
and effectiveness consistent with the highest ideals of the Service. I want to take
this opportunity to pay tribute to him once more for his outstanding contribution
to the security and welfare of the nation, and to commend him for his continuing
devotion to duty in a position for which he has already been awarded the Army's
highest award for this type of service, the Distinguished Service Medal.

END

DISTRIBUTION: Aa, Af, B, D (except Do), E, Ea, Ma, N, Sc, T.
10:00 A.M.

Everything Unified, Everybody Happy

CJCS 201 MacArthur, Douglas

CJCS   (11 Apr 51)   FLASH

CINCFE

FROM CJCS PERSONAL FROM BRADLEY PERSONAL TO MACARTHUR

FOLLOWING STATEMENT IS BEING RELEASED BY THE PRESIDENT COLON QUOTE

WITH DEEP REGRET ITEM HAVE CONCLUDED THAT GENERAL OF THE ARMY DOUGLAS

MACARTHUR IS UNABLE TO GIVE HIS WHOLEHEARTED SUPPORT TO THE POLICIES

OF THE UNITED STATES GOVERNMENT AND OF THE UNITED NATIONS IN MATTERS

PERTAINING TO HIS OFFICIAL DUTIES PD IN VIEW OF THE SPECIFIC RESPONSIBIL-

ITIES IMPOSED UPON ME BY THE CONSTITUTION OF THE UNITED STATES AND THE

ADDED RESPONSIBILITY WHICH HAS BEEN ENTRUSTED TO ME BY THE UNITED NATIONS

CMA ITEM HAVE DECIDED THAT ITEM MUST MAKE ABLE CHANGE OF COMMAND IN THE FAR

EAST PD ITEM HAVE CMA THEREFORE CMA RELIEVED GENERAL MACARTHUR OF HIS COM-

MAND AND HAVE DESIGNATED LIEUTENANT GENERAL MATTHEW BAKER RIDGWAY AS HIS

SUCCESSOR PD PARA FULL AND VIGOROUS DEBATE ON MATTERS OF NATIONAL POLICY

IS ABLE VITAL ELEMENT IN THE CONSTITUTIONAL SYSTEM OF OUR FREE DEMOCRACY PD

IT IS FUNDAMENTAL CMA HOWEVER CMA THAT MILITARY COMMANDERS MUST BE GOVERNED

BY THE POLICIES AND DIRECTIVES ISSUED TO THEM IN THE MANNER PROVIDED BY OUR

LAWS AND CONSTITUTION PD IN TIME OF CIRSIS CMA THIS CONSIDERATION IS

PARTICULARLY COMPELLING PD PARA GENERAL MACARTHUR APOSTROPHE SUGAR PLACE

Document 15a. Bradley's memo to MacArthur relieving
him of command, April 11, 1951. [National Archives]

IN HISTORY AS ONE OF OUR GREATEST COMMANDERS IS FULLY ESTABLISHED PD
THE NATION OWES HIM ABLE DEBT OF GRATITUDE FOR THE DISTINGUISHED AND
EXCEPTIONAL SERVICE WHICH HE HAS RENDERED HIS COUNTRY IN POSTS OF GREAT
RESPONSIBILITY PD FOR THAT REASON ITEM REPEAT MY REGRET AT THE NECESSITY
FOR THE ACTION ITEM FEEL COMPELLED TO TAKE IN HIS CASE PD SIGNED HARRY S
TRUMAN UNQUOTE

Document 15b. Bradley's memo to MacArthur relieving
him of command, April 11, 1951. [National Archives]

"Who does Truman think he is —— the PRESIDENT?"

Document 16. Cartoon, "Who does Truman think he is - the PRESIDENT?", by
Jacob Burck; 1951 (Harry S. Truman Presidential Library). Reprinted with special
permission from the Chicago *Sun-Times*, Inc. © 2001. [National Archives]

Eightieth Congress of the United States of America

At the Second Session

Begun and held at the City of Washington on Tuesday, the sixth day of January, one thousand nine hundred and forty-eight

---

AN ACT

To promote world peace and the general welfare, national interest, and foreign policy of the United States through economic, financial, and other measures necessary to the maintenance of conditions abroad in which free institutions may survive and consistent with the maintenance of the strength and stability of the United States.

Be it enacted by the Senate and House of Representatives of the United States of America in Congress assembled, That this Act may be cited as the "Foreign Assistance Act of 1948".

TITLE I

SEC. 101. This title may be cited as the "Economic Cooperation Act of 1948".

FINDINGS AND DECLARATION OF POLICY

SEC. 102. (a) Recognizing the intimate economic and other relationships between the United States and the nations of Europe, and recognizing that disruption following in the wake of war is not contained by national frontiers, the Congress finds that the existing situation in Europe endangers the establishment of a lasting peace, the general welfare and national interest of the United States, and the attainment of the objectives of the United Nations. The restoration or maintenance in European countries of principles of individual liberty, free institutions, and genuine independence rests largely upon the establishment of sound economic conditions, stable international economic relationships, and the achievement by the countries of Europe of a healthy economy independent of extraordinary outside assistance. The accomplishment of these objectives calls for a plan of European recovery, open to all such nations which cooperate in such plan, based upon a strong production effort, the expansion of foreign trade, the creation and maintenance of internal financial stability, and the development of economic cooperation, including all possible steps to establish and maintain equitable rates of exchange and to bring about the progressive elimination of trade barriers. Mindful of the advantages which the United States has enjoyed through the existence of a large domestic market with no internal trade barriers, and believing that similar advantages can accrue to the countries of Europe, it is declared to be the policy of the people of the United States to encourage these

MAKING PROGRESS

This Government has been informed that a Jewish
state has been proclaimed in Palestine, and recognition
has been requested by the *provisional* Government thereof.

The United States recognizes the provisional government as the de facto authority of the new ~~Jewish~~ *State of*
~~state.~~ *Israel.*

Harry Truman

Approved
May 14, 1948.

6.11

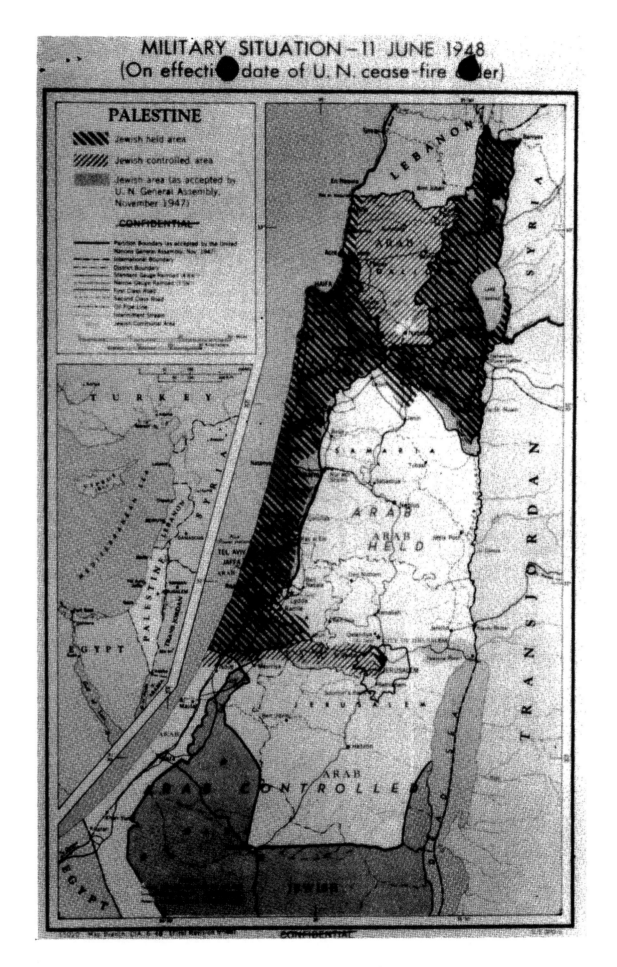

Document 20. Map of Israel's military situation, June 11, 1948. [National Archives]

Document 21. Photograph, "Dr. Ralph Bunche at Arab-Israeli armistice talks,"
1949. © by Bettmann Newsphotos. Used with permission. [National Archives]

JOHN L. McCLELLAN, ARK., CHAIRMAN

JAMES O. EASTLAND, MISS.   JOSEPH R. McCARTHY, WIS.
CLYDE R. HOEY, N.C.   IRVING M. IVES, N.Y.
GLEN H. TAYLOR, IDAHO   KARL E. MUNDT, S. DAK.
HERBERT R. O'CONOR, MD.   MARGARET CHASE SMITH, MAINE
HUBERT H. HUMPHREY, MINN.   ANDREW F. SCHOEPPEL, KANS.
A. WILLIS ROBERTSON, VA.   ARTHUR H. VANDENBERG, MICH.

WALTER L. REYNOLDS, CHIEF CLERK

United States Senate

COMMITTEE ON
EXPENDITURES IN THE EXECUTIVE
DEPARTMENTS

June 3, 1950

Senator Millard E. Tydings, Chairman
Senate Foreign Relations Subcommittee
United States Senate

Dear Mr. Chairman:

Your committee has now been in existence nearly four
months during which time my task of forcing upon you proof of
Communism in the State Department is meeting with more and more
resistance from you and your staff.

I realize that the Lucan-McMahon-Tydings Combine, with
the all-out support of the Administration, feel that your whitewash
will be successful by the use of the following five pronged attack:

(1) To have the President keep under lock and key the
proof while feeding out a few raped and denuded files.

(2) To have you as chairman and your staff go all-out
in an attempt to make it impossible to force proof upon your
committee.

(3) When you are finally forced to accept proof, to
keep secret the evidence which will expose Communists in the State
Department and make public my testimony which will serve to whitewash.

(4) To utilize the State Department's entire press corps
and the Communist's poison-pen artists to attack the wife and family
of any witness who dares to tell the truth about Communists in
government and to attempt to personally destroy such witness.

Document 22a. Senator McCarthy's letter to Senator Tydings
about loyalty investigations, June 3, 1950. [National Archives]

(5) To utilize the vast and expensive press and publicity corps of the entire government to sell the American people the idea that if McCarthy could not succeed in forcing you to make an about-face and accept and make known to the public proof of Communism in the State Department, that then no such proof exists.

Unfortunately, you were having some success in selling that line until a few days ago at which time your staff got carried away by the success of its efforts to date and made the blunder of going too far with a loyal intelligent American who had the guts to strike back. I refer to Mr. Archibald Van Beuren, the top Security Officer of the OSS during wartime -- the man who was in charge of the OSS investigation of Amerasia.

As you recall, months ago I urged the committee to call Mr. Van Beuren, Mr. Frank Bielaski, who made the first raid upon Amerasia, and General Donovan, who was the head of OSS.

I pointed out then that a thorough investigation of the Amerasia case would break the back of the spy ring which extends deep within our State Department. It was only after I went on a radio network and publicly demanded that Bielaski be called that you finally called him. He, of course, was called in secret.

Obviously, Mr. Bielaski had to be discredited if the whitewash were to succeed. Therefore, following the usual tactics of your committee, you called the Justice Department attorneys and made available to the press those parts of their testimony which would tend to discredit Bielaski and still hold secret their cross-examination which sheds some light on the dangerous nature of some of the stolen documents.

Instead of calling Mr. Van Beuren to testify as I had requested, your staff interviewed him in New York, after which the announcement was made that he would not be called to testify.

I thereupon wired Mr. Van Beuren asking him to tell me what happened when your staff called upon him. His answer indicates the fantastic and reprehensible extent to which the whitewash efforts are being carried:

That wire is as follows:

Senator Joseph R. McCarthy
Senate Office Building
Washington, D. C.

Messrs. Tyler and Heald, attorneys for Tydings Committee called on me May 23. I have a strong feeling they were more interested in my reactions to Mr. Bielaski's testimony than they were in my knowledge of early stages of Amerasia case. At no time did they ask for my opinion, as Security Officer of OSS, of the importance of the documents which I saw.

I myself volunteered that I definitely felt their unauthorized possession constituted a threat to national security in time of war. I told them that if the Tydings Committee was interested in that, I would be glad to testify. I could also confirm and supplement Mr. Bielaski's testimony as well as testify to the circumstances which led General Donovan to hand over the documents taken from Amerasia's office to the Secretary of State in person. They said that on the basis of what I told them they felt it was not necessary to call me and they would so recommend.

I feel they were primarily interested in getting information from me which would contradict or possibly discredit Mr. Bielaski's testimony rather than information that would further their investigation of the Amerasia case.

I wonder if the attorneys would have urged that I be called had I contradicted Mr. Bielaski?

Archibald Van Beuren

While I have long known that your staff has been endulging in this type of activity, it is indeed fortunate that the American people can finally get the rather complete and sordid picture thereof.

As you know, I have over a score of witnesses who I had hoped could be presented to your committee. Obviously it would be foolhardy for me to submit them to the type of horseplay and abuse to which my witnesses have been subjected in the past. Unless you give the minority members of the committee the right to subpoena witnesses and develop the facts through their counsel without having them and their employers previously heckled and badgered by your whitewash bucket brigade, I shall be forced to the conclusion that it is worse than hopeless to attempt to force proof upon your committee.

Mr. Tydings, you, Mr. Lucas, Mr. McMahon, the Administration and the State Department's press corps underestimate the intelligence of the American people.

You and Senators Lucas and McMahon backed by all of the power of Washington bureaucracy and its combined highly paid press staff, may convince me of the hopelessness of the further FORCE FEEDING of your committee with distasteful proof of Communism in the State Department. However, you and the Administration can rest assured that no matter how much you try to obstruct the task of exposing people in the government dangerous to this country, you shall not succeed. I assure you that all the power of the Administration won't stop this fight.

Sincerely,

JOE McCARTHY

IN THE UNITED STATES DISTRICT COURT
FOR THE SOUTHERN DISTRICT OF NEW YORK

- X

UNITED STATES OF AMERICA,

     -against-

JULIUS ROSENBERG and ETHEL ROSENBERG,

          Defendants.

C 134-245

(TITLE OMITTED)

- X

Order denying Rosenbergs' Application for Stay - Dec. 10, 19__

     The defendants having moved for an order in open court
on December 10, 1952 staying the execution of the separate
judgments of conviction against them for the crime of conspiracy to commit espionage (Section 34, Title 50, U.S.C.), dated
and filed April 5, 1951 and the order of Hon. Irving R. Kaufman,
Judge of the United States District Court for the Southern
District of New York, dated and filed November 21, 1952,
refixing the date of the execution of the death sentences
imposed under the aforesaid judgments of conviction for the
week commencing January 12, 1953, pending an appeal to the
United States Court of Appeals for the Second Circuit from an
order of Hon. Sylvester J. Ryan, Judge of the United States
District Court for the Southern District of New York, dated
and filed December 10, 1952 denying the application of the
defendants, under Section 2255, Title 28, U.S.C., to set aside
and vacate the sentences of death imposed upon each of them
under the aforesaid separate judgments of conviction, and
staying the execution of the said judgments of conviction and

     AFTER hearing in open court on December 10, 1952,
EMANUEL H. BLOCH, attorney for the defendants in support of
the said application and the United States Attorney for the
Southern District of New York, by JAMES B. KILSHEIMER, Jr.

Assistant United States Attorney, in opposition thereto, and due deliberation having been had thereon, and the Court having found that such appeal presents no substantial question of law, it is

ORDERED that the application of the defendants, JULIUS ROSENBERG and ETHEL ROSENBERG, to stay the execution of the separate judgments of conviction against them for the crime of conspiracy to commit espionage (Section 34, Title 50, U.S.C.) dated and filed April 5, 1951 and the order of Hon. Irving R. Kaufman, Judge of the United States District Court for the Southern District of New York, dated and filed November 21, 1952, refixing the date of the execution of the death sentences imposed under the said separate judgments of conviction for the week commencing January 12, 1953 until the determination of the appeal of the said defendants from the said order of Hon. Sylvester J. Ryan, Judge of the United States District Court for the Southern District of New York, dated and filed December 10, 1952, denying the application of the defendants, under Section 2255, Title 28, U.S.C., to set aside and vacate the sentences of death imposed upon each of them under the aforesaid separate judgments of conviction and denying a stay of the execution of the said judgments of conviction, be and the same is in all respects denied.

Dated: New York, N.Y.
        December 10, 1952.   Sylvester J. Ryan
                                              U.S.D.J.

Document 24b. Court order denying the Rosenbergs' application
for a stay of execution, December 10, 1952. [National Archives]

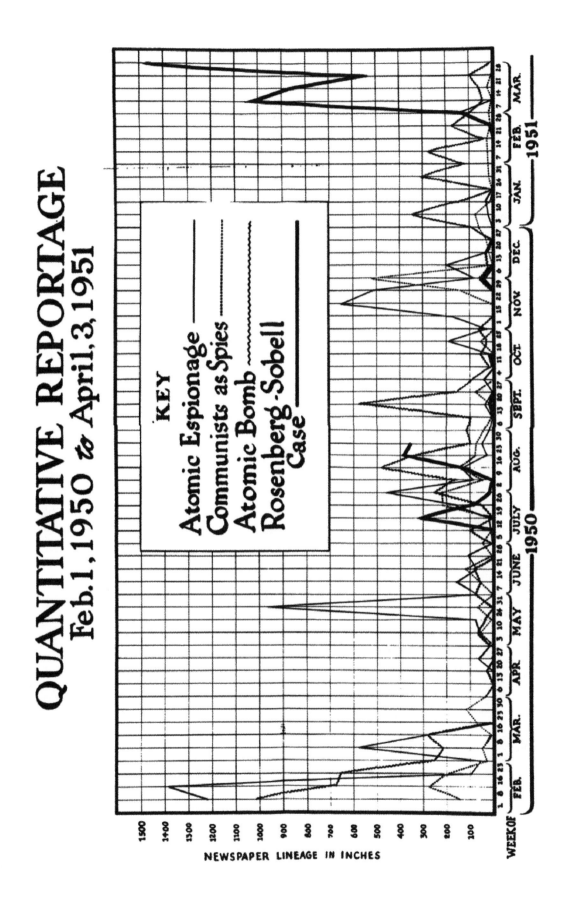

Document 25. Chart of quantitative reportage on the Rosenberg
trial and related espionage topics, 1952. [National Archives]

~~TOP SECRET~~   PARAPHRASE NOT REQUIRED

NR: CA TT 3426

SUBJECT: Korean Situation

REFERENCE: CX-56812; CX-56802.

Conferees:

Washington (CSA)   Tokyo (CINCFE)

From Kearney		
To :		
Adm Radford		
Col. Watson		
Capt. Anderson		
Col. Hutchin		
Cdr. Johnston		
Mr. Kearney		
Maj. Dwyer		
Maj. Carson		
Col Nagle		

Washington (CSA)

Sec Pace, SA
Sec Finletter, SAF
Sec McCone, USAF
Gen Bradley, CJCS
Gen Collins, CSA (mc)
Gen Vandenberg, CSUSAF
Adm Sherman, CNO
Gen Haislip, VISA CSA
Gen Ridgway, DEP CSA
Gen Bolte, G3
Gen Irwin, G2
Mr Bond, STATE

Tokyo (CINCFE)

C/A Douglas MacArthur, CINCFE
Vice Adm C T Joy, COMNAVFE,
Maj Gen E M Almond, C/S FEC
Maj Gen C A Willoughby, G2 FEC
Maj Gen G L Eberle, G4 FEC
Maj Gen W A Beiderlinden, G1 FEC
Maj Gen D O Hickey, DEP C/S FEC
Maj Gen A F Fox, DEP C/S SCAP
Maj Gen E E Partridge, ACTO CGFEAF
Brig Gen E K Wright, G3 FEC
Brig Gen G I Back, SIG O FEC
Col L J Fortier, G2 FEC
Lt Col J H Chiles, SGS FEC

Washington: DA-1

President has directed that instructions be issued as
follows:

All restrictions on employment of FECOM Navy and Air
Forces are removed. They will offer fullest possible support to South Korean forces so as to permit these forces to
reform.

Purpose of above action is to support SK forces in
accordance with resolution of United Nations approved 25 June.

In addition 7th Fleet will take station so as to prevent invasion of Formosa and to insure that Formosa not be
used as base of operations against Chinese mainland.

Detailed instructions reference Navy and Air Forces
follow:

DA TT 3426   (JUN 50)

OCS FORM 375-4 REPLACES OCS FORM
375-4 1 MAR 46 WHICH
MAY BE USED. OCS FORM 21, 15 DEC
45 WHICH MAY BE USED.

Document 26a. Teletype of Truman's authorization of military
intervention in Korea, June 27, 1950. [National Archives]

CLASSIFIED
TELETYPE
MESSAGE
CONFERENCE

TOP SECRET
STAFF COMMUNICATIONS OFFICE
DEPARTMENT OF THE ARMY
STAFF COMMUNICATIONS OFFICE

TOP SECRET

NR: DA TT 3426   PAGE 2

All restrictions which have previosly prevented the full utiliza tion of the U.S. Far East Air Forces to support and assist the defense of the South Korean territory are lifted for operations below the 38th Parallel. All North Korean tanks, guns, military columns and other military tar- gets south of the 38th Parallel are cleared for attack by U.S. Air Forces. The purpose is to clear South Korea of North Korean military forces. Similarly Naval Forces may be used without restriction in coastal waters and sea approaches of Korea south of 38th Parallel against forces engaged in aggression against South Korean. (End DA-1)

Washington: DA-2.

Imperative that you use every method available to you to advise Amb Muccio, Korean military leaders and Korean civilian officials of these decisions as they relate to Korea. (End DA-2)

Washington: DA-3.

What is your latest information summary of military situation in Korea? (End DA-3)

Tokyo: FEC Item 1.

Summary situation since 270145I last report CK 56812. Chief KMAG quotation N-Koreans have capability to take Seoul within 24 hr i.e Tuesday/Wednesday. S-K C/S takes attitude that the fall of Seoul is fall of South Korea. Latest info to 10 A.M. Tokyo time: Piecemeal entry into action North of Seoul by South Korean Third and Fifth Divisions has not suc- ceeded in stopping the penetration recognized as the enemy main effort for the past 2 days with intent to seize the capital city of Seoul. Tanks entering suburbs of Seoul. Government transferred to south and communication with part of KMAG opened at Taegu.

South Korean units unable to resist determined northern offensive. South Korean casualties as an index to fighting have not shown adequate resistence capabilities or the will to fight and our estimate is that a complete collapse is possible. (End item 1)

Washington: DA-4.

What means of communications do you have now with Korea? (End DA-4)

DA TT 3426   (JUN 50)

Document 26b. Teletype of Truman's authorization of military intervention in Korea, June 27, 1950. [National Archives]

PROCLAIMING THE EXISTENCE OF
A NATIONAL EMERGENCY

BY THE PRESIDENT OF THE UNITED STATES
OF AMERICA

A PROCLAMATION

WHEREAS recent events in Korea and elsewhere constitute a grave threat to the peace of the world and imperil the efforts of this country and those of the United Nations to prevent aggression and armed conflict; and

WHEREAS world conquest by communist imperialism is the goal of the forces of aggression that have been loosed upon the world; and

WHEREAS, if the goal of communist imperialism were to be achieved, the people of this country would no longer enjoy the full and rich life they have with God's help built for themselves and their children; they would no longer enjoy the blessings of the freedom of worshipping as they severally choose, the freedom of reading and listening to what they choose, the right of free speech including the right to criticize their Government, the right to choose those who conduct their Government, the right to engage freely in collective bargaining, the right to engage freely in their own business enterprises, and the many other freedoms and rights which are a part of our way of life; and

WHEREAS the increasing menace of the forces of communist aggression requires that the national defense of the United States be strengthened as speedily as possible:

NOW, THEREFORE, I, HARRY S. TRUMAN, President of the United States of America, do proclaim the existence of a

Document 27a. Proclamation by Truman of a national
emergency, December 16, 1950. [National Archives]

national emergency, which requires that the military, naval, air, and civilian defenses of this country be strengthened as speedily as possible to the end that we may be able to repel any and all threats against our national security and to fulfill our responsibilities in the efforts being made through the United Nations and otherwise to bring about lasting peace.

I summon all citizens to make a united effort for the security and well-being of our beloved country and to place its needs foremost in thought and action that the full moral and material strength of the Nation may be readied for the dangers which threaten us.

I summon our farmers, our workers in industry, and our businessmen to make a mighty production effort to meet the defense requirements of the Nation and to this end to eliminate all waste and inefficiency and to subordinate all lesser interests to the common good.

I summon every person and every community to make, with a spirit of neighborliness, whatever sacrifices are necessary for the welfare of the Nation.

I summon all State and local leaders and officials to cooperate fully with the military and civilian defense agencies of the United States in the national defense program.

I summon all citizens to be loyal to the principles upon which our Nation is founded, to keep faith with our friends and allies, and to be firm in our devotion to the peaceful purposes for which the United Nations was founded.

I am confident that we will meet the dangers that confront us with courage and determination, strong in the faith that we can thereby "secure the Blessings of Liberty to ourselves and our Posterity."

Document 27b. Proclamation by Truman of a national emergency, December 16, 1950. [National Archives]

IN WITNESS WHEREOF, I have hereunto set my hand and caused the Seal of the United States of America to be affixed.

DONE at the City of Washington this *10:20 A.M.* day of *Dec. 16, 1950.* December in the year of our Lord nineteen hundred and fifty, and of the Independence of the United States of America the one hundred and seventy-fifth.

Harry S. Truman

By the President:

Dean Acheson

Secretary of State

27 March 1951

MEMORANDUM FOR THE SECRETARY OF DEFENSE

        Subject: United States Position Regarding
                     an Armistice in Korea.

    1. In the course of the meeting on 19 March 1951 which
you attended with the Secretary of State and the Joint Chiefs
of Staff, the question was posed by the Secretary of State as
to whether or not the armistice terms, as set forth in the
memorandum to you from the Joint Chiefs of Staff dated 12
December 1950, were still valid.

    2. The Joint Chiefs of Staff, from the military point
of view, have formulated the following views on the broader
problem of the termination of hostilities in Korea which
supersede the views furnished you in their memorandum dated
12 December 1950.

    3. The Chinese Communists and the North Korean forces
are now suffering especially heavy losses. Any arrangement
which did not prejudice their position in Korea but which
would end the infliction of large losses on the Communists
would be greatly to their advantage. Conversely, an arrangement which would require United Nations forces to remain in
Korea, and which did not prejudice the position of the Communist forces there, would be greatly to our disadvantage.
Such an arrangement would, in all probability, jeopardize
the security of our forces, constitute an unwarranted drain
on our military resources, and tie down our forces in Korea
almost as effectively as if they were engaged in combat.
From the military point of view, therefore, an armistice
arrangement of itself would not, even temporarily, constitute an acceptable solution of the Korean situation.

    4. The Joint Chiefs of Staff consider that the present
military situation in Korea may be conducive to a satisfactory
resolution of the immediate over-all problem by political
action. Specifically, it may be possible to take political
action to end the aggression, to conclude the fighting and

insure against its resumption. Such a resolution of the
situation, however, must provide for a termination of
hostilities in Korea only under circumstances which would
make possible the ultimate attainment of our objective without forfeiture of, or prejudice to, our general position
with respect to the USSR, and with specific respect to
Formosa, and to seating the Chinese Communists in the
United Nations.

5.   In view of the foregoing, any armistice arrangement must, from the military point of view, be contingent
upon the acceptance of a general agreement which protects
the over-all security interests of the United States.
Therefore, the Joint Chiefs of Staff cannot concur in any
armistice agreement which does not include the terms, conditions, and arrangements set forth in paragraphs 6 and 7
below, and particularly in subparagraph 6 a. Further,
these must be agreed to by all governments and authorities
concerned, including North Korea and Communist China, prior
to the implementation of any armistice arrangement.

6.   The armistice arrangement:

a. Must be contingent upon the acceptance by the
Communists of a general agreement to end the aggression
and to accept basic terms of settlement (satisfactory to
the United States;) *stated below;*

*You can say the
same thing w/o
the irritating par-
enthetical phrase*

b. Shall be confined to Korea;

c. Shall require all governments and authorities
concerned, including North Korea and Communist China,
to order a cessation of all acts of armed force; the
establishment of a demilitarized area across Korea;
and all ground forces to remain in position or be
withdrawn to the rear except that all forces which
may be in advance of the demilitarized area shall be
moved to positions in the rear thereof;

d. Shall provide for supervision of the general
arrangements, as well as specific details, by an
Armistice Committee (under a Peace Commission designated by the General Assembly of the United Nations),
which Committee shall have free and unlimited access
to the whole of Korea. This Committee may, if necessary, be assisted by a limited number of observers
designated by the Chinese Communist and/or North
Korean forces;

Document 28b. Joint Chiefs of Staff memo to Secretary of Defense regarding
Korean armistice proposals, March 27, 1951. [National Archives]

    e. Shall require all governments and authorities concerned to cease promptly the introduction into Korea of any reinforcing units or personnel, including volunteers, during the armistice period. This shall not be interpreted as precluding the administrative relief of individual personnel on a man-for-man basis;

    f. Shall require all governments and authorities to refrain from introducing additional war equipment and material into Korea. Such equipment and material will not include those supplies required for the maintenance of health and welfare and such other supplies as may be authorized by the Committee; and

    g. Shall continue in effect until the details of a permanent settlement of the Korean situation have been arranged.

7. The Joint Chiefs of Staff consider the following specific details to be essential to the above armistice arrangement:

    a. The Armistice Committee must be competent to inspect to insure that the terms, conditions and arrangements as agreed to will be carried out by all armed forces, including guerrillas in Korea. It shall be provided with a sufficient number of competent military observers to enable it to carry out its duties and functions;

    b. Its provisions should not become effective until the Committee has been organized and is in position to exercise its functions. The Committee shall report promptly to the General Assembly of the United Nations all violations of the armistice arrangement;

    c. The demilitarized area shall be a zone on the order of 20 miles in width, centered at or north of the 38th parallel. Its exact location shall be determined by the Armistice Committee on the basis of the position of the opposing ground units in combat at the time;

    d. The armistice arrangement shall apply to:

TOP SECRET

Document 28c. Joint Chiefs of Staff memo to Secretary of Defense regarding Korean armistice proposals, March 27, 1951. [National Archives]

(1) All opposing ground forces in Korea, wherever located. In addition, those forces shall respect the demilitarized zone and the areas in advance thereof;

(2) All opposing naval forces in the Korean area which shall respect the waters contiguous to the land areas occupied by the opposing armed forces, to the limit of three miles offshore. Naval units designated by the Committee for sea transport, supply, evacuation, surveillance, and humanitarian purposes shall be excepted from the foregoing provision while such units are engaged in these duties and have on board a representative of the Committee; and

(3) All opposing air forces which shall respect the air space over the demilitarized zone and the areas in advance thereof. Air units designated by the Committee for air transport, supply, evacuation, surveillance, and humanitarian purposes shall be excepted from the foregoing provision while such units are engaged in these duties and have on board a representative of the Committee.

e. Teams of military observers appointed by the Committee together with such United Nations Armed Guards as may be available and considered appropriate by the Committee shall have freedom of movement anywhere throughout all Korea;

f. Prisoners of war shall be exchanged on a one-for-one basis as expeditiously as possible;

g. Organized bodies of armed forces initially in advance of the demilitarized zone shall be moved back or passed through to the area of their own main forces. Guerrillas, both north and south of the demilitarized zone, shall be withdrawn and be granted safe conduct through the demilitarized area under terms and conditions to be established by the Committee;

h. Nothing in the agreement shall preclude commanders in the field from providing for the security of their forces, supplies, and installations, except that no security forces for this purpose will be permitted within the demilitarized area;

Document 28d. Joint Chiefs of Staff memo to Secretary of Defense regarding Korean armistice proposals, March 27, 1951. [National Archives]

<u>i</u>. The Committee shall be responsible for civil government, including police functions, in the demilitarized zone; and

<u>j</u>. Refugees shall not be allowed to migrate in either direction into or across the demilitarized area.

For the Joint Chiefs of Staff:

HOYT S. VANDENBERG,
Chief of Staff, United States Air Force.

Document 28e. Joint Chiefs of Staff memo to Secretary of Defense regarding Korean armistice proposals, March 27, 1951. [National Archives]

Document 29. Photograph of President Truman campaigning in California,
September 24, 1948 (Harry S. Truman Presidential Library). [National Archives]

Document 30. Cartoon, "—— and on Two Legs," Nov. 3, 1948
(Harry S. Truman Presidential Library). © *Evansville Courier.*
Used with permission. [National Archives]

ASOCIACION DE INDUSTRIALES DE PUERTO RICO
Y ASOCIACIONES AFILIADAS

ASOC. FABR. PERFUMERIA Y. ALCOHOLADO
FELIX HILERA, Presidente

ASOC. DE FABRICANTES DE MUEBLES Y PRODUCTOS DE MADERA
PEDRO SARKIS, Presidente

ASOC. DE EMBOTELLADORES DE GASEOSAS
CHARLES T. MOCK, Presidente

ASOCIACION DE TAHONEROS
SANTIAGO PIÑERO, Presidente

SALON DE ACTOS Y OFICINAS CRUZ NO. 250 — APTDO. 2227 — TEL. 2-4451 — SAN JUAN DE PUERTO RICO.

JUNTA GENERAL DE DIRECTORES

*

ANGEL SUAREZ
PRESIDENTE

JOSE CARRERAS
VICE-PRES.

JOSE NOVAS
TESORERO

VICENTE LEON, JR.
SECRETARIO

*

VICE-PRESIDENTES DE DISTRITO:

JUAN SUAREZ
SAN JUAN

M. A. MAYORAL
PONCE

R. RODRIGUEZ SCHETTINI
MAYAGUEZ

JOSE V. OLIVER
ARECIBO

JOSE OCHOA
GUAYAMA

J. M. GONZALEZ SILVA
AGUADILLA

S. JIMENEZ SOLIS
HUMACAO

*

DIRECTORES DE DISTRITO:

POR SAN JUAN:
SANTOS ZUBILLAGA
PEDRO SARKIS

POR PONCE:
JUAN VAZQUEZ VELEZ
JOSE ROVIRA JR.

POR MAYAGUEZ:
GILBERTO E. RODRIGUEZ
GABRIEL SOLER

POR ARECIBO:
AMELIO CORTEZ
RAMON MA. BRAVO

POR GUAYAMA:
PEDRO ANIBARRO
MANUEL PEREZ

POR AGUADILLA:
JOSEPH C. LAWS
ROBERTO ESTEVES

POR HUMACAO:
ANGEL ALONSO
ANGEL ALGARIN

*

PRESIDENTE HONORARIO:
J. A. E. RODRIGUEZ

CONSEJERO:
TEODORO MOSCOSO, JR.

November 8th, 1950.

Hon. Harry S. Truman
Washington, D. C.

Dear Mr. President:

    This Association which represents a large majority of the manufacturing industries of Puerto Rico wishes to express to you its deep regret for the action of two irresponsible and fanatically minded Puerto Ricans who tried to force their way into Blair House with the intention of harming your Excellency.

    As your Excellency is well aware of the feelings of the majority of the Puerto Ricans, we will not repeat here what thousands of telegrams and letters have already expressed to you. It is a sad thing, however, that while thousands of Puerto Ricans are at present fighting under the American flag for democracy in Korea, a few fanatics, who are so few in number that they are not taken seriously even by their own countrymen, should give the false impression to the mass of the American people that the Puerto Ricans are disloyal to you and to the American institutions that you represent.

    We, as well as the immense majority of the Puerto Ricans, would like the American people to know that the sentiments of our people are represented by the men now fighting side by side with our fellow citizens of Continental United States in the Far East.

    We wish to express to you our rejoicing that the attack upon your person was frustrated, and pray that God may keep your life and health in these moments of great concern for our Nation.

Respectfully yours,

ASOCIACION DE INDUSTRIALES DE P.R.

By: *Angel Suárez*
Angel Suárez, Pres.

AS:anv

Document 31. Suarez's letter to Truman about the attempted assassination, November 8, 1950 (Harry S. Truman Presidential Library). [National Archives]

COUNCIL FOR CIVIC UNITY
215 W. 7th Street
Los Angeles 14, California
Trinity 6271

Dr. E. C. Farnham
President

March 15, 1946

G. Raymond Booth
Executive Secretary

Mr. Aaron Riche
Treasurer

Dr. Laurence I. Hewes, Jr.
American Council on Race Relations
Regional Director
259 Geary Street
San Francisco 2, California

Dear Doctor Hewes:

I will attempt to give you herewith some rather scrappy bits of information
and impressions concerning the employment conditions in Los Angeles as they affect
minority groups. I have talked at length with persons in positions of leadership
among the several minorities and also persons in public service. I think it should
be said with a great deal of emphasis that practically no one has any information
to which they would assign their names. Part of this state of affairs is because
voluntary organizations are not properly financed and staffed to enable them to
engage in even the most elementary forms of research. Part of it is due to the
fact that the United States Employment Service in particular seems to feel that
it should not give out information except through regular channels. It would
be impossible, therefore, in all cases to give credit to my sources.

There are perhaps 205,000 Negroes in Los Angeles County. These are the
figures used by Army Intelligence. The Urban League estimates the number at
150,000. I am not sure how the Army arrives at its figures. The Urban League
makes its estimate partly on the traffic load in the office and partly from deductions in connection with the U.S.E.S. information. I am inclined to think there
are about 150,000 in the city with only a few thousand outside the city limits.
San Pedro, for instance, has about 5,000, all of whom are in-migrants. A few
have been just outside the County. Pasadena has always has a small Negro con-
stituency which has been enlarged somewhat during the war. Long Beach had had
a sizeable in-migrancy. Glendale, as usual continues to be "lily-white."
There is a small Negro community in the northeast part of the San Fernando
Valley. On should be definitely aware of the fact that Negro in-migrancy continues pretty much unabated. Negro GIs are coming in from the South to take
advantage of educational opportunities.

There are perhaps 235,000 persons of Mexican ancestry in the county,
most of them east of Main Street. There are, however, some Mexicans in the
Santa Monica and in the Agricultural areas withint the city limits between

downtown Los Angeles and the harbor. The term, "wet Mexican," long in use in Texas, is now being heard here much more frequently. The term is used to denote Mexicans who originally crossed the Rio Grande illegally with the connivance of Americans who sought their labor. In addition there is a sizeable evaporation from the Mexican National camps with, so far as I have been able to discover, no official investigation.

Jewish sources would indicate that there are approximately 168,000 Jews in Los Angeles.

The Washington office of the War Relocation Authority uses the figure 16,000 as the number of Japanese American returnees. The local office here uses 25,000. The Washington office arrives at its figure by adding all the local estimates throughout the country, discovered that that totals about twice the number of Japanese in America, and then makes its deductions. The local office has an involved method of figuring it on the basis of traffic load in the office, which is not very convincing. Perhaps there may be 20,000. All other persons of Oriental ancestry constitute a much smaller number.

The outlook for jobs for Negroes is distinctly not good. I am sure Mr. Ross has access to official U.S.E.S. reports or he can get them. I suspect that they will show that as of about a month ago at least 22 per cent of all employer orders placed are discriminatory in character. This will not give the total amount of discrimination for two reasons: (a) records I think are quite incomplete and (b) there is no breakdown to indicate the number of orders for employees invoved in discriminatory as opposed to non-discriminatory orders. Mr. Raymond Krah, who has been dealing with a very vocal deputation of Negro leaders recently was quoted in the Leftist press as saying 70 per cent of employer orders were discriminatory in character. I can discover no indication that U.S.E.S. has established any priority for firms whose orders are non-discriminatory. Casual observation at the U.S.E.S. office at 11th and Flower, together with inquiries elsewhere would indicate that the applicant load ranges from 50 per cent to 80 per cent Negro in a city where less than 10 per cent is Negro. This would seem to indicate a very high proportion of Negroes who become unemployed will not be able to get jobs, at least through ordinary channels.

One usually very reliable source indicates that we have about returned to prewar status in types of industrial jobs now open to Negores. In other words, that most of the gains which have been made during the war have been lost, or are in process of being lost. Heavy work, hazardous work and dirty work in iron and steel are still open to Negroes, but not much else. Even jobs which have been considered as the prerogative of Negroes are being challenged, since we have moved into a Classification IV status, namely, in the service trades. Employers who have taken untrained Southern whites into even such jobs as dishwashers find that they are thereby unable to employ Negroes. Clerical and commercial jobs where the workers deal with the public are practically nonexistent.

The main opportunities for Negroes are in such boom trades as textiles. The charge is made, and I think with some degree of justification, that more Negroes cannot be employed in office positions or in technical positions because they are not qualified. The joker, of course, is that they do not have the opportunities to learn such skills because they could not be employed anyway. Attempts on the part of U.S.E.S. to get employer cooperation have been met, I am informed, with a good deal of resistance, even to the point of cancellation of job orders. My information is that the M. and M xxx is the chief source of organized non-cooperation with U.S.E.S. on such matters as the above-named problems.

Information regarding Mexican Americans is conceded by everyone to be the most fragmentary. There is not an aggressive Mexican leadership. Complaints from Mexican sources to F.E.P.C. did not at all reflect the amount of discrimination. Mexicans did not make the same advance during the war as did the Negroes. Futhermore, they are much more inclined to accept their fate as being inevitable. In employment Mexicans are under the same handicaps as are Negroes. What small advances the Mexicans made was in the main due to the vacuum created by the evacuation of Japaneese Americans. This gain they are now in the process of losing. A recent formation of a Mexican Civic Affairs Committee offers some hope, but not much.

The return of the Japanese Americans has been far more successful than many people believe possible. However, the success, where there has been success, has been due much more to their own initiative than to any help either from the W.R.A. or from citizen organizations. Those who had homes, farms, professional status and some capital have been able to establish or re-establish themselves fairly well along the traditional lines of Japanese occupation. There are at least 4,000 returnees who are now stranded as to housing and income except for completely undesirable public installations operated by the F.P.H.A. and some dozen or more hostels operated by private committees. The hostels and installations are too remote from job offerings for those who are able to work. Relief case load is now well over a thousand, involving perhaps 4,000 persons. A wide variety of job opportunities for American citizens of Japanese ancestry which were developed in the middle west and east are largely non-existent here. The old stereotypes quite largely persist. The one bright spot in Japanese American employment has been the large number of openings for girls in clerical and other office work. Perhaps the least excusable attitude toward Japanese American employment is on the part of the Federal Government and the State government. Both the County and City public service have better records.

Racial tensions in connection with employment is not yet as acute as it undoubtedly will be when a large number of persons of minority groups come to the end of their unemployment insurance payments and are unable because of discrimination to secure suitable re-employment. Furthermore, the chief source of racial tension in this city grows out of the indignity of restrictive covenants. Some persons in the field of housing are sure that there are among the minorities at least 140 families for each 100 units of family housing. At least 50 per cent, and perhaps nearer 75 per cent of the total overloading of housing units was directly chargeable to restrictive covenants.

Sincerely,

G. Raymond Booth
Executive Director

EXECUTIVE ORDER

ESTABLISHING THE PRESIDENT'S COMMITTEE ON EQUALITY OF TREATMENT AND OPPORTUNITY IN THE ARMED SERVICES

WHEREAS it is essential that there be maintained in the armed services of the United States the highest standards of democracy, with equality of treatment and opportunity for all those who serve in our country's defense:

NOW, THEREFORE, by virtue of the authority vested in me as President of the United States, by the Constitution and the statutes of the United States, and as Commander in Chief of the armed services, it is hereby ordered as follows:

1. It is hereby declared to be the policy of the President that there shall be equality of treatment and opportunity for all persons in the armed services without regard to race, color, religion or national origin. This policy shall be put into effect as rapidly as possible, having due regard to the time required to effectuate any necessary changes without impairing efficiency or morale.

2. There shall be created in the National Military Establishment an advisory committee to be known as the President's Committee on Equality of Treatment and Opportunity in the Armed Services, which shall be composed of seven members to be designated by the President.

3. The Committee is authorized on behalf of the President to examine into the rules, procedures and practices of the armed services in order to determine in what respect such rules, procedures and practices may be altered or improved with a view to carrying out the policy of this order. The Committee shall confer and advise with the Secretary of Defense, the Secretary

of the Army, the Secretary of the Navy, and the Secretary of the Air Force, and shall make such recommendations to the President and to said Secretaries as in the judgment of the Committee will effectuate the policy hereof.

4. All executive departments and agencies of the Federal Government are authorized and directed to cooperate with the Committee in its work, and to furnish the Committee such information or the services of such persons as the Committee may require in the performance of its duties.

5. When requested by the Committee to do so, persons in the armed services or in any of the executive departments and agencies of the Federal Government shall testify before the Committee and shall make available for the use of the Committee such documents and other information as the Committee may require.

6. The Committee shall continue to exist until such time as the President shall terminate its existence by Executive order.

Harry Truman

THE WHITE HOUSE,
    July 26, 1948.

Document 34. Photograph of Jackie Robinson, 1950. © Bettmann
Newsphotos. Used with permission. [National Archives]

Rests With Other Heroes; Indian Sergeant Is Buried In Dignity, With All Honor

Arlington National Cemetery, Va. Sept. 5—(UP)—Sgt. John R. Rice, American Indian who was denied a grave in his hometown's "all white" cemetery, was buried among the nation's war heroes today with all the honor and dignity his first funeral lacked.

It was the Army's way of making amends to a fighting infantryman who served throughout World War II in the Pacific and died defending the Pusan bridgehead in Korea last September 6.

Sergeant Rice's first funeral, in Sioux City, Iowa, was halted at the graveside last week, after "taps" had been sounded and the casket was ready to be lowered. Officials of the Memorial Park Cemetery said they had just learned he was "not a member of the Caucasian race."

Sergeant Rice's 29-year-old white widow, Evelyn, and his invalid 65-year-old mother, Mrs. Sammie Davis, had no such humiliation to undergo today. They were joined at the graveside by Oscar Chapman, Secretary of the Interior; two Senators, Guy M. Gillette (D. Iowa), and Hugh Butler (R. Nebr.). Maj. Gen. Charles D. Palmer, Sergeant Rice's commander in Korea, and more than 400 other mourners.

President Truman, who personally arranged the Arlington burial, sent a large wreath of pink and white flowers, and an Army Colonel to represent him.

Racial segregation once prevailed in Arlington, just as it does today in most private cemeteries in Sioux City, Washington and a great many other cities. But since 1947, all American soldiers have been equal in death in Arlington, and no distinction is made between the graves of officer and enlisted man, white and colored races.

Sergeant Rice's grave, on a grassy knoll overlooking the Capital, is less than 100 yards from that of another Korean war casualty—Gen. Walton H. Walker, Commander of the Eighth Army.

The flag-draped casket, which arrived from Sioux City Monday, was removed from a vault in the Ft. Myer, Va., chapel shortly before 11 a. m. and placed on a black artillery caisson drawn by seven matched gray horses.

An Army band with muffled drums and muted horns led the half-mile procession to the grave, playing "Holy, Holy Holy."

The caisson was followed by an honor guard of six sergeants from the Third Infantry Regiment who gave up three-day passes to volunteer for the duty. One of them was Sgt. George Osborne, a half Cherokee Indian.

Another honor guard, from the American Legion, followed the automobile which carried the widow, mother and other relatives and friends brought here at Army expense.

Capt. John F. Orzel, a Ft. Myer Chaplain, conducted the brief, solemn Catholic internment rites, in Latin and English. He prayed that Sergeant Rice might "rest in peace" and invoked a blessing on the grave.

The only eulogy was General Palmer's quiet statement to reporters:

"I knew him in Korea. He was a fine soldier. He did a good job."

Mrs. Davis, sitting in a wheelchair, removed her tortoise-shell glasses to wipe her eyes. And the widow sobbed softly as they heard—for the second time in a week—the crack of rifles firing a three-round volley over the grave, and the mournful notes of "Taps."

This time, they could be sure, was the last time. The casket was lowered into the grave, and the flag which covered it was folded by the honor guard and handed to the widow.

Sgt. John R. Rice, American hero, had found a last resting place, and his nation had made its humblest apologies to his memory.

Document 35. "Rests With Other Heroes; Indian Sergeant Is Buried in Dignity, With All Honor," *The Cincinnati Enquirer*, September 5, 1951 (Harry S. Truman Presidential Library). [National Archives]

Document 36. Photograph of a housing project, 1946
(Harry S. Truman Presidential Library). [National Archives]

Document 37. Photograph of the interior of prefabricated government housing,
May 3, 1949 (Harry S. Truman Presidential Library). Reprinted by permission of
the William H. Harmon Corporation of Wilmington, DE. [National Archives]

Document 38. Advertisement for television, February 13, 1950 (Harry S. Truman Presidential Library). © Motorola Inc. Used with permission. [National Archives]

Document 39. Advertisement for Lustron home, 1950
(Harry S. Truman Presidential Library). [National Archives]

Document 40. Photograph of Erikson Oil Products station, North
Lyndale, Minneapolis, December 29, 1954. [National Archives]

Teaching With Documents Order Form

The Truman Years: 1945-1953

You may order copies of the following document in its original size:

Document	Price	Qty.	Total
Document 25. *(17x22, b/w)* Chart of quantitative reportage on the Rosenberg trial and related espionage topics, 1952.	$24.00		
Add 5% MD Sales Tax (if applicable)			
Shipping & Handling (Ground Shipping: $10.00, Air Shipping: $22.00)			
Total			

Billing Address:

_____

_____

_____

_____

Shipping Address: (if different from Billing Address)

_____

_____

_____

_____

☐ Check Enclosed payable to Graphic Visions Associates

☐ VISA   ☐ Mastercard   ☐ American Express

_____/_____/_____/_____/   _____/_____   _____
Credit Card Number   Exp. Date   Authorized Signature

(_____)_____   (_____)_____
Telephone   Fax

Mail Order To: Graphic Visions
640 East Diamond Avenue, Ste. F
Gaithersburg, MD 20877